creatingcustomerevangelists

How Loyal Customers Become a Volunteer Sales Force

BEN McCONNELL | JACKIE HUBA

Dearborn™
Trade Publishing
A **Kaplan Professional** Company

This publication is designed to provide accurate and authoritative information in regard to the subject matter covered. It is sold with the understanding that the publisher is not engaged in rendering legal, accounting, or other professional service. If legal advice or other expert assistance is required, the services of a competent professional should be sought.

Vice President and Publisher: Cynthia A. Zigmund
Editorial Director: Donald J. Hull
Acquisitions Editor: Mary B. Good
Senior Project Editor: Trey Thoelcke
Interior Design: Lucy Jenkins
Cover Design: Jody Billert
Typesetting: the dotted i

Published by Dearborn Trade Publishing
A Kaplan Professional Company

Printed in the United States of America

03 04 05   10 9 8 7 6 5 4

Library of Congress Cataloging-in-Publication Data

McConnell, Ben.
    Creating customer evangelists : how loyal customers become a volunteer
sales force / Ben McConnell, Jackie Huba.
        p.   cm.
    Includes bibliographical references and index.
    ISBN 0-7931-5561-4
    1. Customer relations.   2. Relationship marketing.   I. Huba, Jackie.
II. Title.
HF5415.5 .M1834 2002
658.8—dc21
                                                                          2002012221

dedication | **For our parents—Matt and Betty, John and Kass**

CONTENTS

FOREWORD

After we launched the Macintosh in 1984, hundreds of Macintosh user groups sprang up around the world. They were gatherings of passionate believers who helped each other become better Mac users. They sustained Macintosh when Apple couldn't—or wouldn't.

Don't get me wrong: We didn't know what we were doing. This stuff was just happening, and we did our best to keep "it" happening, where "it" = "Create unbelievably loyal customers and ignite a holy war between operating platforms."

After this experience, I wrote *Selling the Dream* to evangelize evangelism. But that was 1989, and it was a different marketing world. We didn't have the Internet, 500 channels of cable TV, satellite radio, or cell phone spam.

Now the entire world is drenched and debauched in content and advertising, and we need evangelism even more. We sure don't need more stinkin' ads. We need more folks who spread the good news. This customer religion is built on great products and services. The next step is fueling the fire of customer love, and this is what this book explains.

There are four reasons why the evangelistic customer approach is important: (Some readers will know that I usually deliver such pronouncements in a top ten format, but considering that this is a foreword and space is limited, I'll keep it short.)

1. It's cheap. You don't need to pay evangelists. Most of the time, you just need to get out of their way.
2. It's effective. Think about the last significant purchase that you made: What was the biggest influence? Probably the word-of-mouth reputation of the product, not a Super Bowl commercial.

3. It's fun. How much better can it get than working with people who love your product or service and want to help make the world a better place?

4. It will drive your competition crazy when they see hundreds or thousands of customers turn into raging thunderlizards for your products and services.

Those are some of the key lessons you'll learn from *Creating Customer Evangelists*. I wish I had written this book, but I'm glad that I didn't have to, because writing a good foreword is a lot easier than writing a great book.

Guy Kawasaki
CEO
Garage Technology Ventures
Palo Alto, California

ACKNOWLEDGMENTS
it takes a community

Writing a book requires a tremendous level of collaboration from multiple sources, some of which are named in the chapters of this book. Others played behind-the-scenes, yet vital, roles.

We are very grateful for the assistance of the leaders of our case story companies and their teams. They devoted many hours of what probably seemed an endless array of interviews, e-mails, phone calls, and fact checking. We are thankful to:

Maxine Clark, Teresa Kroll, and Katy Hartrich of Build-A-Bear Workshop.
Mark Cuban, Matt Fitzgerald, George Killebrew, and George Prokos of the Dallas Mavericks.
Stan Parker, Ashley Neighbors, and Brooke Smith of Krispy Kreme Doughnuts.
Tim O'Reilly, Mark Brokering, Catherine Brennan, Sara Winge, and Sandy Torre of O'Reilly & Associates.
Gerald Haman of SolutionPeople.
Jim Parker, Kevin Krone, Linda Rutherford, and Patty Kryscha of Southwest Airlines.

The following people took the time to talk with us about many concepts in the book: Richard Alm, Jeffrey "Hemos" Bates, Chris Bontrager, Jeanne Cusick, Brian Erwin, Melissa Giovagnoli, Alex Johnston, Guy Kawasaki, Evelyn McClure, Ann McGee-Cooper, Rich Marcotte, Karen Mishra, Kevin Olsen, Emanuel Rosen, Heath Row, Liz Ryan, Tim Sanders, Jackie Sloane, Daryl Urquhart, and Todd Walley.

We are extremely thankful to a stalwart group of friends and colleagues who reviewed our manuscript and made it more readable. Our thanks go to Lynn Barney, Nancy Cobb, Kevin Dowling, Betsy Harman, Kass Huba, John Huba, Dan Limbach, Matthew Lindenburg, Betty McConnell, Matthew McConnell, Lynne Marie Parson, and Simone Paddock. Their thoughts, ideas, and suggestions helped us tremendously; any errors or omissions rest solely with the authors. We'd also like to thank Victoria Rock and Tara Bonaventura of Victoria's Transcription Service for their timely help. We are thankful to our editor, Mary B. Good, for taking a chance on first-time authors. We appreciate the support of Leslie Banks and Elizabeth Bacher of Dearborn Trade.

Even though this section is becoming about as long as an Academy Awards speech, we want to publicly thank several other gracious friends who helped us and have evangelized our work to the world: Donna Itzoe, Greg Heaps, Liza Ewell, Lee Mann, Simone Paddock, Richard Landman, Todd Hassell, Tonja Rizai, Kathleen Peterson, Betsy Harman, and Melissa Giovagnoli. We also thank the accommodating staff of Starbucks Coffee at North Avenue and Wells in Chicago, where we spent several hundred hours writing and editing this work.

We'd like to acknowledge two women who, over the last year, showed us what the power of evangelism is all about: Lynne Marie Parson and Stacey Wagoner. Thanks for your enthusiasm and support. Thanks to authors Emanuel Rosen and Dan Pink for their wisdom and guidance, and to Guy Kawasaki for being an inspiration.

CHAPTER 1

CUSTOMER EVANGELISM
a manifesto

"We are encouraging our clients to fly Southwest Airlines. We are buying more stock . . . and we stand ready to do anything else to help. Count on our continuing support."[1]

—SOUTHWEST AIRLINES CUSTOMER ANN MCGEE-COOPER,
in an October 2001 letter to Southwest President Colleen Barrett

You are an evangelist.

You tell others what movie to see, which computer to purchase, what restaurant to visit, which dentist you prefer, which cell phone to buy, which books to read, which clubs to join. Your recommendations are sincere. Passionate, perhaps.

Perhaps you didn't realize that you are an evangelist—a bringer of glad tidings—but your sphere of influence, made up of friends, family, colleagues, and professional communities, realizes it.

As our opening quote indicates, Ann McGee-Cooper is a Southwest Airlines customer who stands by a company she loves. After the September 11, 2001, attacks, which crippled and jeopardized airlines for months, McGee-Cooper wrote the company, informing it that she was persuading clients, friends, and family members to fly Southwest Airlines and was purchasing tickets on their behalf. She bought the company's stock. Perhaps most tellingly, she included a $500 check with her letter, saying that the airline needed the money "more than I do."[2]

She is more than a loyal customer; she is a *customer evangelist.*

A loyal customer is often defined as one who buys from you on a regular basis. If you're an airline, loyal customers are usually defined as those who accumulate the most frequent-flyer miles. If you're a grocery store, a flower shop, or a café, perhaps your loyal customers are those who live within walking or easy driving distance. Their loyalty to you may be driven by convenience or low prices. In effect, they are repeat customers, not necessarily loyal customers.

A repeat customer who purchases on the basis of convenience or low cost can easily morph into a vigilante customer, one who spreads the word about your deplorable service to all who will listen. Once this begins, your share of customers' wallets begins to decline along with their goodwill.

Customer evangelism spreads by word of mouth. It spreads by word of mouse via e-mail and the Internet. This is known as buzz, a potent and cyclical phenomenon. Buzz lives and dies in a predictable, bell curve model that helps to create new customers or turn off potential ones. A customer evangelist is like a friend you've known for years whose relationship helps support your organization through good times and bad.

What does a customer evangelist look like? How do you know if someone is extolling your virtues? These are the attributes of customer evangelists:

- They purchase and *believe in* your product and or service.
- They are loyal and passionately recommend you to friends, neighbors, and colleagues.
- They purchase your products as gifts for others.
- They provide unsolicited feedback or praise.
- They forgive occasional dips in service and quality but let you know when quality slips.
- They are not bought; customer evangelists extol your virtues freely.
- As your evangelist, they feel connected to something bigger than themselves.

The lessons from the original evangelists—the religious believers who roamed the backstreets of the world to spread the word of their faith—teach us that beliefs are based on emotional connection, deep-seated convictions, and the promise of a better way. Strongly held beliefs compel many of us to tell others. The root of the word *evangelist* is based on "a bringer of glad tidings."

But this book is not about religion. It's about how the traditional rules of marketing are changing. It describes how traditional marketing and advertising tactics are declining in their effectiveness and how customer-driven referrals are the valuable new currency in a company's success. This book is about how future customers often first hear about you from a trusted friend or family member. It describes how evangelists are key influencers on future customers and how customers may have been enlisted on your behalf well before you knew what was happening.

Think about the last time one of your friends gushed about a product. Perhaps it was about a movie, a restaurant, a new toothpaste, or even an attorney. For the purpose of demonstration, let's say the product was a new hair-straightening iron. You and your friend would rather have straight hair than the curly locks you were born with, so you must resort to mechanical means.

Your friend's story probably followed these steps:

1. A description of what she bought
2. How she bought it
3. Why she bought it
4. How she has used it
5. How it has affected her and what it means to her

If she's a potent evangelist, her eyes light up and her voice is tinged with emotion. You may say, "Wow, this sounds pretty good. I'll have to try it." Because you know her and trust her, you're connected to her and her story. You remember her story the next day and can repeat it almost verbatim.

When you see your friend a few weeks later, she asks if you've had a chance to try the product she'd mentioned. "Not yet," you say. Her reply: "We are going to make a date this weekend, and I am going to show it to you myself." She is instinctively leading you through the sales process, generating enthusiasm, overcoming objections, and perhaps closing the deal.

Your friend is a customer evangelist, a volunteer salesperson. Customers like her help companies because they love to help other people by using a great experience of their own. Often, they may also want to help you and your company succeed. You have helped them, so they want to return the favor. They feel an intrinsic human desire to repay you.

In this book we examine large, medium, and small companies in different industries to find how they have created customer evangelists. Our research shows that customer evangelism exists beyond demographic and ethnographic groups, product categories, or types of services. Using an in-depth case story approach, we introduce you to the customer evangelism that's happening with:

- Southwest Airlines
- Krispy Kreme Doughnuts
- Build-A-Bear Workshop
- Dallas Mavericks
- O'Reilly & Associates

- SolutionPeople
- IBM

You'll discover how customer evangelists want others to benefit as they have. You'll discover how evangelists influence and, in some cases, become part of a company's volunteer salesforce. Perhaps most important, we discuss the ways you can create evangelists for your company.

The impetus to write this book grew from our experiences in evangelizing products and services. Both of us are avid readers, and we found ourselves impulsively telling others about our new favorite books. For two years in the late 1990s, we interviewed hundreds of applicants for our fast-growing company. We evangelized *Customers.com*, by Patricia Seybold, and *Futurize Your Enterprise*, by David Siegel, to many of the applicants as well as to our colleagues. Because those books had an impact on us, we wanted others to share in that knowledge. We helped Seybold and Siegel sell several hundred copies of their books; and, in fact, a colleague who took our recommendation bought 50 copies of Siegel's book as presents for prospective clients. Witnessing that act codified the power of everyday evangelism.

Our book seeks to shed light on this marketing phenomenon. During times of recession, one of the first departments usually cut in a business is marketing. The recession of 2000–2002 was no different. Two million people were laid off in the United States.[3] A record 257 publicly traded companies filed for bankruptcy in 2001, representing a 46 percent increase over the prior year's record of 176 filings.[4]

Yet some businesses rode out the recession without layoffs (or with only minimal furloughs), steady profitability, and minimal budget cuts, if any. These standout companies were successful despite economic turmoil. In researching this phenomenon, we discovered similarities in the customer base of seven separate companies: Each had spent previous years maniacally focusing on delighting customers and building loyal, passionate fans who would continue to support the business through times of economic distress.

In studying these companies, we discovered a series of common approaches they shared, which we have distilled into six tenets. These are the six tenets of customer evangelism:

1. Customer Plus-Delta: Continuously gather customer feedback.
2. Napsterized knowledge: Make it a point to share knowledge freely.
3. Build the buzz: Expertly build word-of-mouth networks.
4. Create community: Encourage communities of customers to meet and share.

5. Make bite-size chunks: Devise specialized, smaller offerings to get customers to bite.
6. Create a cause: Focus on making the world, or an industry, better.

These tenets can be applied across small, medium, and large businesses in any industry.

The seven companies we studied are leading their industry's efforts in creating customer evangelists. We interviewed their customer evangelists, their CEOs, and their marketing executives. Many told inspiring stories about their dedication to customers and how their efforts are often driven by "just doing the right thing." Our case stories look at the people behind the company and their approach to customers as well as the lessons they can teach all of us.

A note: Although many in business today consider the job of acquiring and retaining customers to be one for the marketing department, we found that the companies we studied assign that responsibility to the entire organization. That philosophy emanates consistently from the top down, not the bottom up or somewhere in between. If we examine a growing movement in software technology—the open source community where developers from multiple companies and countries collaborate to create software standards and products—we discover a key lesson. Author Eric S. Raymond describes the breakthrough for open source as happening because "a strategic decision-maker got the clue and then imposed that vision on the people below him."[5]

As such, this book is more than a resource for marketing leaders; it is a guide for all leaders to make their organizations more customercentric, no matter whether the customer is a consumer, a client, another business, or a citizen.

WHAT'S WRONG WITH MARKETING TODAY?

> *"Who's to blame/for this state of distress?*
> *It's the Marketing Director! We all confessed."*[6]
>
> —FROM THE SONG "LET'S ALL BLAME THE MARKETING DIRECTOR,"
> by Harpell

If it's not the messenger that companies shoot first, then it's the marketing director. In 2001, Harpell, a Massachusetts ad agency, surveyed prospective technology marketing managers to discover their pains. Respondents said, "My budget's been cut but I have to produce more"; "I'm on my way out the door"; "My staff's been cut." It was a bleak report. As part of a marketing campaign to promote its services, Harpell produced an old-timey, saloon-style song accompanied by a plunky piano about the trials and tribulations of a marketing director who is continually blamed for lack-luster sales. Harpell reminds us that whether it's the marketing director's fault or not, that person usually takes the bullet for disappointing sales.

Why? Let's examine today's marketing environment. How can marketers create successful, innovative programs in a business environment that punishes risk and makes the marketing department the scapegoat for any stupid decision ever made? Let's explore what's wrong with marketing.

Marketing in 2002 is based on 1960's principles.

What's taught in a college marketing class? The four Ps: Product, Place, Price, and Promotion—a concept introduced by E. Jerome McCarthy in 1960. In 2002, most marketing education programs are still based on the four Ps. Promotion, the fourth of the four, is all about advertising, sales promotion, public relations, and personal selling. Most college marketing textbooks cover very little, if anything, about word-of-mouth and customer evangelism.

Marketing is advertising.

The next time you're at cocktail party, ask someone for the definition of *marketing*. Chances are he or she will say it's advertising. Worse yet, your imbibing test subject may define marketing as telemarketing, which is really caveman marketing in our view.

Unfortunately, the common definition of marketing is what we are bombarded with everyday: advertisements. In his book *Data Smog*, author David Shenk surmised that the average person is exposed to more than 3,000 advertising messages per day.[7] Our senses are under continual assault, much of it by bad or useless information.

There are other subtle instances of how marketing has been co-opted by advertising. For example, Jim Kirk's thrice-weekly column, "On Marketing, Etc.," in the *Chicago Tribune* is mostly about the extensive Chicago advertising industry. Because he focuses almost exclusively on mass media ad campaigns developed by Chicago shops and the high level of turnover in those agencies, the column is really "On Advertising, Etc."

Which marketing professionals are glamorized in the media? Ad executives. Remember the devious ad agency owner played by Heather Locklear on the television show *Melrose Place?* How about the lead characters on the show *thirtysomething?* Dustin Hoffman was the beleaguered father and ad agency executive in the Oscar-winning film *Kramer vs. Kramer.* The Darrin Stevens character from the popular *Bewitched* TV sitcom was an ad man. Ad execs, all of them! When was the last time a customer service manager was the hero of a blockbuster film? Don't answer that.

Power goes to those with the biggest budgets. How do some marketing managers measure their success in the corporate hierarchy? By the size of their marketing budgets. A former brand manager for a large consumer packaged goods company told us that a big marketing budget is about coalescing internal power; helping customers solve problems is not necessarily at the top of the list. At some large companies, you had better spend all of your annual budget or you'll receive less money next year.

What's the fastest way to spend money? Mass advertising. What incentive does an ambitious marketer have for creating customer evangelists and word-of-mouth programs that cost dramatically less? None, unless you enjoy being passed over for promotions. Unfortunately, many marketers are promoted and hired on the basis of the budget they grew and managed, not on the results they delivered.

Marketing must produce results now, damnit. We are an instant gratification society. We want our food fast and our Internet connections blazing. Why pay cash when credit is easier? So it goes for marketing. The stock market rewards companies for growing revenues and profits quarter by quarter. Wall Street shows little interest in long-term investment. Wall Street doesn't want to hear about money spent on customer evangelism programs. Investment bankers care about one thing only: how many new customers you will generate in the next 12 weeks.

Revenues down? The Street wants to know what actions you are going to take now. Layoffs? Good, they'll say. Wall Street rewards layoffs with a stock price bump. Sales are slipping? Hey you, marketing director, forget that customer satisfaction study. Just get those print materials for the field salesforce—and while you're at it, start a new and more aggressive telemarketing campaign!

Marketing is desperate. The globalization of commerce has produced an economy rich with choices. How do we decide, really, between 165 cereal products and 85 different breakfast bars? Right now, there are ads for a multitude of products on television and buses, under computer browser windows, in the waiting rooms of physicians and dentists, on phone cards, on the backs of lottery tickets, and on banners towed by noisy planes circling around crowded beaches, annoying people trying to get away from it all. At 3,000 advertisement exposures per day, *that's 188 messages per hour, three per minute every minute of every day.*

With so much competition, mass media ads must scream louder and more often just to squeeze through the clutter. In 1980, ad agency pioneer David Ogilvy argued that ads must run at least nine times before a future customer grasps your message. Of course he would! He was an ad executive who made money from the size of your ad budget and the number of times you ran your ad. Some call this interruption marketing, but it's really desperation marketing. The mass advertiser pleads with you to please, please, please . . . nine or more times, actually . . . buy! Continuous repetition of mass media ads signals desperation, a sign that nothing else is working.

If a company cannot differentiate its products or focus on a specific target audience, then it usually settles for advertising the lowest price, the last refuge of a company that has lost its way.

Marketing to new customers is sexy. Evidence shows that acquiring a new customer is five times more expensive than keeping a current customer happy. Moreover, customer profitability tends to grow the longer a customer stays with you; it costs less to keep a customer coming back for more. Yet we see many otherwise bright, college-educated marketers spend millions of dollars on advertising, direct mail, and a black hole from outer space known as "branding"—all in the name of acquiring new customers. Why?

It's the thrill of the chase. The opening scene in *Kramer vs. Kramer* shows Dustin Hoffman accepting congratulations from his ad agency peers; he happily says that landing the coveted $2 million Revlon account was "one of the five best days of my whole life." Landing new customers is sexy, like cavemen slaying a gazelle on the grasslands. Keeping current customers, like gathering nuts and berries or growing a garden, is hard work.

Mass marketing is dying. Response rates for several campaign tactics continue their inevitable decline. Measures of the average Internet banner click-through range from 0.005 to 1 percent. The average direct mail response rate is 1 to 2 percent. Response rates for television and print advertising remain unclear; and measures such as "brand awareness" and "purchase intent" are vacuous at best.

Consider the results of a study released in 2001 by Euro RSCG Worldwide, one of the largest advertising agencies in the world, regarding the influences on buyers of consumer technology products. It found how consumers get most of their information about technology products:

- 13 percent from advertising
- 20 percent from Web sites
- 34 percent from word of mouth

What "generated excitement" about a tech product or service?

- 0 percent from radio
- 1 percent from billboards

- 4 percent from TV ads
- 4 percent from print ads
- 15 percent from magazines
- 40 percent from referrals by colleagues or family[8]

Times change, and it's time for marketing tactics that worked for past generations to evolve from a model predicated on advertising and direct mail to one based on building customer goodwill. The continuous, mind-numbing marketing repetition that clogs the arteries of our attention every day is like one of the common definitions of insanity: doing the same thing over and over again and expecting different results.

* * *

What we have learned so far is that traditional message platforms are so crowded as to be ineffective. We have learned that marketing principles in 2002 are based on ideas that are at least 40 years old. Their effectiveness has been diluted by exponential growth of a media-driven culture, the ubiquity of information sources, and since 1994, the advent of the World Wide Web.

How do we evolve from the primordial ocean of advertising? How do we help our best customers become our best salespeople? By developing an understanding of when customers believe.

WHEN CUSTOMERS BELIEVE

"Sales is rooted in what's good for me. Evangelism is rooted in what's good for you."[1]

—GUY KAWASAKI, author of *Selling the Dream* and *Rules for Revolutionaries*

Do your customers recruit new customers on your behalf?

Do your customers provide you with ideas for new products, product improvements, new services, store locations, or new strategies that would work with their business partners?

Customer evangelists do all of these things. Focusing your business and your marketing on creating evangelists is the most profitable approach to acquiring and retaining customers.

In most businesses, the marketing group is typically responsible for activities that acquire and retain customers. But why? Smart business leaders know that marketing is more than a department; it's a philosophy and belief system for the entire organization, like a corporate religion, and the strongest believers are the best leaders. This is a truism for creating employee evangelists as much as customer evangelists.

Companies that create organizational charts, business plans, and mission statements around the customer—not around their own internal structure—are ones that tend to create sustainable, long-term value. So evangelize this book to your CEO, COO, customer service reps, and field salesforce.

Customer evangelism is a philosophy about customers. Inside a business thriving with customer evangelists, everything is designed to keep customers coming back. These companies deliver memorable experiences that compel customers to share their knowledge with others. Leaders who believe in customer evangelism marketing rely on more than the four Ps, segmentation, distribution channels, advertising, direct mail, and the like. They earn their trophy shelf positions because they focus on learning everything possible about customers and interact with them more than their competitors do.

As we spoke with the leaders of our case story companies, we discovered a pattern: most said their approach was about "doing the right thing." Even the biggest of the big said their marketing strategy wasn't anything out of the ordinary. Not once did we encounter a strong emphasis on "creating shareholder value" as the rallying cause of our case story companies. This is not to diminish the importance of shareholder value, but companies that engineer plans and tactics with shareholder value and growing their stock prices at double-digit rates as their primary belief systems actually engineer themselves toward the deep hole filled with the likes of Enron, Arthur Andersen, Global Crossing, Sunbeam, WorldCom, and a thousand misguided dot-coms. Greed is not good.

Repeatedly, we found that our case story companies develop *relationships* with customers, often a reflection of the company's culture. (This is different from CRM, or customer relationship management, which tends to wrongly imply that a multi-million-dollar investment in a CRM software package creates better customer relationships.) A customer evangelism philosophy based on customer relationships is embodied in the belief system of the company founder or chief executive.

Employees in our case study companies—from Southwest's 33,000 employees to SolutionPeople's 10—believe in the company's core philosophy toward customers and practice it. To understand a company's culture, look at its chief executive: Is he a people person? Does she focus on building relationships inside and outside the company? Approachable or untouchable? Down to earth or imperialistic?

Other questions: Does the chief executive ooze ostentation with gold cufflinks and $1,800 tailored suits? Or does he seem like a neighborly guy who would happily loan you his lawnmower?

If you are the chief, do you enjoy the people part of the job? Be honest: If dealing with people consistently annoys you, then you're in the wrong job, because your philosophy and nonverbal language about relationships spread to all departments beyond the marketing group. The chief executive's personality becomes the organization's personality. How the chief executive works with people is often a reflection of how a company treats its customers.

Most people in business are committed to the customer in spirit but lack the tools and tactics to fully embrace this commitment. Upcoming chapters discuss models for creating customer evangelists and present good, practical advice from companies that succeed at creating customer evangelists.

WHEN EVANGELISM FIRST MET BUSINESS

The popularization of evangelism in business can be traced to Guy Kawasaki and Apple Computer in the 1980s. Kawasaki was named a "software evangelist" in 1983, and his job was to sell the Macintosh dream to developers who would write software for the Apple computer. The dream was to increase the productivity and creativity of people using personal computers.

The Macintosh was a revolutionary product for its ease of use and unique design, drawing favorable reviews from early customers. The fervor and zeal of software evangelists like Kawasaki fostered an image of a company that wanted to change the world.

Kawasaki says that Apple realized its approach had a secondary effect on its business. "The job title [of evangelist] already existed at Apple when I got there, so I didn't invent the title," he says. "It was used more in the evangelistic sense of preaching, pounding on the pavement, getting the job done, taking the battle to the customer—all that stuff.

"The secondary effects of getting people to believe, who then got more people to believe, is something that was stumbled upon. In my recollection, I was never told, 'OK, you go get XYZ to write software, and they in turn will get more customers to buy your software and to buy Macs. We never thought it through that much. That's what happened, but that was not the plan."[2]

The company created so many accidental customer evangelists that they organized themselves into user groups. "Apple has thousands of user groups," Kawasaki says. "Those are truly the evangelists. They're not paid. They're not employees. They tell people to use Macintosh solely for the other person's benefit. That is the difference between evangelism and sales. Sales is rooted in what's good for me. Evangelism is rooted in what's good for you."[3]

With the Internet, the impact of customer evangelism grew exponentially. Two components of evangelism—word of mouth and buzz—became part of the popular marketing vernacular. Hotmail, the free e-mail service, is the well-known poster child for word-of-mouth marketing. Hotmail grew to 12 million subscribers in 18 months, thanks to strong word of mouth. The Hotmail phenomenon was deemed "viral marketing" because of its ability to "infect" potential customers with marketing the product itself. Hotmail did this by putting "Get your free e-mail at Hotmail.com" at the bottom of every e-mail.

By accident or by design, customer evangelism is organic in nature. It's grass roots. It sprouts from the customer level and begins to bloom with customers talking with one another.

WHY CUSTOMER EVANGELISM WORKS

Customer evangelism is the most effective form of advertising available —and it's mostly free. Customer evangelism works for five reasons.

1. The volunteer salesperson is a trusted friend or advisor.
2. The advice is coming from an independent source, not the manufacturer.
3. The message is usually genuine and free of hype.
4. The value of the product or service is personalized for the recipient.
5. The referrer explains the value until it's fully understood by the recipient.

As a marketer, entrepreneur, or something in between, your job is to help those naturally occurring roots grow deeper. Customer evangelism cuts through the muck of advertising clutter. Friends, family, and colleagues influence our behavior more than any repetitive ad or aggressive salesperson can.

Why are customer evangelists the ultimate salespeople?

- They know your target audience better than you because they *are* the target audience.
- They can search out and find others just like themselves faster and easier than you can.
- They know what your prospective customers do for a living.
- They know where your prospects live.
- They translate your value proposition into words the prospects will understand.

Great customer evangelists follow up with a prospect after they make their evangelistic pitch and help close the sale. Some offer to drive the new customer to the store to help buy the product.

Customer evangelism reduces the time it takes for a prospect to make a purchase decision. George Silverman outlines this concept in *Secrets of Word-of-Mouth Marketing:* purchasing a product or service is not a single decision but a series of decisions. "If you can identify and minimize just a few of those decision bottlenecks for your customers, you can reduce their decision time by more than half, thereby multiplying the sales and market share of your product or service," he writes.[4] Customer evangelists nurture a prospect through the decision cycle to complete the purchase.

CUSTOMER EVANGELISM MARKETING AS A PRACTICE

The purpose of Customer Evangelism Marketing is to create customer evangelists who spread the good word about your products and services. An organization with a Customer Evangelism Marketing program focuses all external and internal activities on this common objective. We have identified three keys to a successful program.

1. A Great Product or Service

What makes a product or service great? Greatness is in the eye of the customer, but here are some common themes to consider. (*Note:* throughout this book, we try to use the words *product* and *service* interchangeably as we do *he* and *she*.)

Using what we call the SEAMS model, here are the aspects of a great product or service:

- Satisfies a customer need, want, or desire
- Easy to use (A great product is also easy to find and purchase.)
- A good value—a subjective measure defined by the customer but ultimately is the customer's belief that the benefits of the service are worth the money
- Makes the customer's life better, improving the personal or professional condition of the purchaser
- Solves a customer problem that sometimes the customer didn't know he had

How do you know if your products and services are great? Ask your customers! Ask what they love about your products or services. Ask what they say when they tell others about them. Begin by looking for what they say on Internet bulletin boards and in discussion groups.

Quality alone doesn't guarantee success. The landscape of business history is littered with superior, Goliath products defeated by more nimble and popular Davids. Sony's Betamax system and IBM's OS/2 operating system were superior compared with their competition: high quality and state of the art. But JVC's VHS system and Microsoft's Windows won because of expert marketing.

Some people believe that as long as the end result is high quality, people will spread the word about it. This is true—but only to a point.

2. A Maniacal Focus on Customers

Most marketers and business executives contend they are focused on customers. We understand that the purpose of business is to satisfy customer needs, yet many of us don't walk the talk. Do you? Take the following quiz.

Have you visited with a customer in the past 30 days?	Yes	No
Do you gather some form of customer input every month?	Yes	No
Can you describe, in detail, your ideal customer persona (not a demographic)?	Yes	No
Do you have a customer satisfaction program?	Yes	No
Is employee compensation tied directly to customer satisfaction?	Yes	No
Do you know your average customer's lifetime value?	Yes	No
Does your organization focus on creating memorable customer experiences?	Yes	No
Do your customers feel they are part of your extended family?	Yes	No
Are employees empowered to do the right things for customers?	Yes	No
Are your customers, suppliers, and employees really treated honestly and fairly?	Yes	No

How did you score?
8–10: Congratulations; you are on your way to creating customer evangelists. You have the foundation for a Customer Evangelism Marketing machine.
4–7: You have the right steps but not the rhythm. It will take some work.
0–4: It's time to get customer religion or wallow in obscurity.
(The appendixes in this book will assist you in putting these ideas into action.)

3. Understanding That Business Is about People

In the halcyon days of the Internet bubble, the focus was on IPOs (initial public offerings), valuations, stock options, and GBF (get big fast). In the recession that followed the bursting of the Internet bubble, businesses slashed costs and focused on improved operational efficiency. Management by spreadsheet took over. The I-told-you-so's said it was time to "return to basics"; *Business 2.0* aptly termed it "The Return of the Crappy Job."[5]

As Tim Sanders, author of *Love Is the Killer App*, says, "The next big thing is . . . people."[6] Sanders implores "bizpeople" to share their knowledge, networks, and compassion. He's right. Treat your customers like your best friends; best friends support you through good times and bad.

Smart marketers eschew the "Art of War" as a pretense for business and embrace "The Loyalty Effect." Successful companies "date" their customers. They ask permission to build a relationship with future customers instead of segmenting them into soulless demographic groups with campaigns to capture them like prey.

Let's look at how one company dates future customers. FranklinCovey, a personal and organizational effectiveness firm located in Salt Lake City, Utah, offers a series of valuable e-mail newsletters written by several of its senior partners called *Helping Clients Succeed.* Free to subscribers, the newsletters offer salespeople detailed tips on developing relationships that ultimately result in sales. FranklinCovey gets instant feedback from readers on each newsletter by including a "Rate this" button in every e-mail. By requesting people to provide their e-mail address in exchange for useful information, the company has really asked permission to make its prospective customers aware of its fee-based seminars and training classes.

FranklinCovey's strategy of building relationships, by offering value up front, positions it well for creating customer evangelists. FranklinCovey Vice President Mahan Khalsa is highly visible in his e-mails. We have gotten to know his warm and witty voice, literally and figuratively. His picture accompanies every e-mail, and we recognize his face with its distinctively long gray beard. Because it seems we have gotten to know him personally, he seems real and trustworthy. He is reducing the number of decisions we must make because of our growing virtual relationship with him.

The odds of looking into Mahan's wise, smiling face and clicking on the "unsubscribe" link? Unlikely. The odds of attending his training class? Very likely. A key point: We haven't purchased anything from FranklinCovey yet, but because we have received value from the organization, we evangelize it.

Marketers often refer to "increasing brand loyalty" as a factor in increasing sales. But does this terminology really make sense? A company and its logo are inanimate. The notion that people are loyal to brands may make some sense for consumer products that have little differentiation: think Evian versus Pellegrino. But, in general, people are loyal to people. Any business in which human beings are involved in selling or delivering a product or service has the ability to significantly influence customer experiences, thereby engendering loyalty.

Phone companies consistently rank lowest for customer service because their monthly bills are purposely complicated and undecipherable. They force customers to navigate a dozen voice menus before reaching a live person. They make customers hang up and dial another number just to talk to another department. Good God, people, you're the phone company . . . fix your phone systems!

When you think of your favorite restaurant, you probably remember the pleasant wait staff or the scowling host as much, if not more, than the food. You may love the location of your apartment, but the responsiveness of the landlord and/or maintenance crew influences your decision to renew or cancel your lease as much as the monthly rent.

Customer evangelism is based on loyalty to people, not things.

GETTING STARTED WITH CREATING CUSTOMER EVANGELISTS

Many common marketing tactics continue to decline in effectiveness but still command the majority of marketing budgets. In 2001, Pepsi hired teen pop star Britney Spears to launch a multi-million-dollar advertising campaign, one of the most expensive in the company's history. One year later, Pepsi sales were down 1 percent,[7] a significant percentage in an industry where market share is measured in decimal points.

Leaders of small companies network like crazy, collect business cards by the bushel, and launch attacks of spamlike direct mail, e-mails, and phone solicitations. This approach creates a few leads and a sleazy reputation. Bury these bad marketing habits six feet under and replace them with customer evangelists. Here's a starter kit of how to do it.

Free yourself from the four Ps. The traditional marketing P for *promotion* usually involves one-way communication: advertising on TV, print, and radio; blast-faxing press releases; and a blizzard of direct mail. Rethink promotion as a two-way process. Seth Godin's *Permission Marketing* details a new approach to the back-and-forth dialogue with prospective customers that Godin likens to dating. Most people can't convince strangers in a bar to marry them; the same is true with ads that ask you to buy *now*. Godin prescribes offering incentives to entice customers to opt in to a conversation. Over time, a customer learns about your product or service and enjoys the budding relationship. The key is conversation, not self-promotion.

The best things in life are free. Pretend you have no marketing budget. (Maybe you don't have to pretend.) Word of mouth and evangelism are gifts that customers give you, but you must first earn them, for money doesn't buy goodwill. The easy approach to marketing is spending money on "branding" ads and direct mail. Instead, work harder to understand what customers love and thereby earn their admiration. Customer evangelism is worth its value in public relations alone.

Dump Wall Street and focus on the long term. Fred Reichheld's *The Loyalty Effect* explains why companies should focus on long-term loyalty: 15 percent lower operating costs than those of comparable companies and growth rates that are 220 percent above average. Quarterly sales quotas are important but not when they drive companies to take a short-term view of taking care of customers. Focus on creating loyal customers; they are your evangelism candidates and customer evangelists will support you in the long run, in good times and bad.

Get out of the cold; go where the heat is. Finding new customers is key to a new and growing business. But how do you find them? Let's begin by dissecting a few simple sales terms.

- *Cold calls.* They're cold. Impersonal. Unexpected. Jarring.
- *Warm leads.* They're inviting. Promising. Feel good.
- *Hot prospects.* They're hot! The customer is ready to buy now or get started yesterday.

Our sales vocabulary is visually descriptive for a reason, so why not spend more time focusing on your existing customers? Customers who love you generate the most heat for your business. Fan the flames. Deepen those relationships. Make sure customers love you, and then tactfully ask if they will open their networks and refer you to others. You may be pleasantly surprised to discover how some customers will help you find warm leads.

Believe in your customers. If you are the analytical type, Customer Evangelism Marketing may seem idealistic and nebulous. You are probably more comfortable approving a numbers-driven approach: A marketing campaign to capture new customers costs $75,000, which sends 100,000 direct mail pieces to a rented list, resulting in 250 warm leads, which results in ten new customers who spend $20,000, returning $200,000 of new revenue. It's easy to calculate that return on investment (ROI).

So how do you calculate the indifference, and perhaps the ire, of 90,000 people whom you have just spammed? How do you calculate the cost of a vigilante prospect who brandishes your direct mail piece as a stellar example of wasteful paper usage?

Evangelism marketers spend their budgets seeking permission to develop relationships with customers, knowing that the investment over time will result in higher profits and lower operating costs. Companies that choose Wall Street as their dance partner often leave customers on the sidelines. Wall Street bankers are like carnival barkers: They are loud, colorful, and entertaining, but they care only about how much money you will make for them.

At times it's difficult to develop a return on investment based on customer evangelism tactics, such as helping the community and hiring genuinely happy and pleasant customer service representatives. But evangelism marketers steadfastly believe that doing the right things for customers will reward them tenfold with repeat purchases and customers who buy from them because of the word of others. It is a leap of faith, just as it is a leap of faith for the analytical type to trust the list broker to deliver a solid list and the creative team to create a solid design.

* * *

As we searched for companies that successfully create customer evangelists, we looked at many industries, including those selling to consumers and businesses. We looked at small, one-person companies, the heavyweights in the Fortune 500, and companies in between. Six common themes emerged in our examination of how these businesses acquired and retained customers, although their specific approaches are quite different.

At their foundations, these companies know what their customers say about them. They encourage customer participation and feedback. Their methods vary, but their intent is consistent: They need to understand the love and the areas for improvement. They have mastered the art of Customer Plus-Delta: the first of the six tenets of evangelism marketing.

CUSTOMER PLUS-DELTA
understanding the love

"Opportunities are often missed because we are broadcasting when we should be listening."

—AUTHOR UNKNOWN

Listen to your customers.

The lessons of the case story companies in Chapters 9 through 16 teach us that listening to customers is a key component to creating customer evangelists. Many of our profiled organizations receive 100s or even more than 1,000 e-mails a day from customers that are filled with suggestions, complaints, and praise. Overwhelming? No way, say the leaders we talked with. They wouldn't have it any other way. To them, a deluge of e-mail confirms that their customers really care.

Our term for gathering feedback is *Customer Plus-Delta*. The *Plus* indicates an understanding of what works well. The *Delta* symbolizes what needs to be improved. Performing a customer plus-delta at various customer touch points gathers quantitative and qualitative data about your organization's performance that can create a big-picture view of how your organization is really performing at the customer level.

Almost every marketing person agrees that customer input is important. It is (or should be) the basis for many of your organization's strategic decisions. However, ask most marketers if they routinely gather feedback, and many times the answer is, "We don't have enough money in our budget to do market research."

It seems the prevailing opinion on performing customer research is that it costs a lot of money, takes a lot of time, and requires too many resources. Common customer feedback tactics include focus groups, customer satisfaction surveys, comment cards, ethnographic studies, qualitative research, and quantitative research. For many organizations, these tactics require considerable work, resources, and time. We discovered with our case story companies that gathering continuous customer feedback is easier and less expensive than you might think.

The most customer-oriented organizations use deceptively simple tactics to understand what customers are thinking. They understand the domino effect of customer satisfaction. Research conducted in the 1980s and 1990s by TARP, a customer loyalty research firm, shows that satisfied customers tell an average of 5 to 8 people about their experience with a company or a product; dissatisfied customers tell 10 to 16 people.[1]

For some perspective, let's use TARP's formula to understand the exponential potential of unhappy customers. We'll use the lower ranges for argument's sake. Let's say you have 1,000 customers whose satisfaction you gauge using a survey tool. Enter your own organization's satisfaction figures to understand the effect.

How to measure the buzz of happy and unhappy customers

Total number of customers	1,000
% of satisfied customers	62%, or 620
Satisfied referrals	620 × 5
Total Happy Referrals	3,100
% of dissatisfied customers	38%, or 380
Dissatisfied referrals	380 × 10
Total Unhappy Referrals	3,800

This chart shows that more than one-half of the referrals for your company can be negative, even though only one-third of your customers are dissatisfied.

With the Internet, these results can be significantly higher. Web sites such as epinions.com and PlanetFedeedback.com are entirely dedicated to encouraging customers to spread the word, often negatively, about any organization. Often, a marketer's perception is that customers are satisfied if they do not complain, but this perception can mask a more common phenomenon: inertia.

Why then don't unhappy customers complain?

- It's hard.
- It takes time.
- They're uncomfortable delivering criticism.
- They don't expect results from their efforts.

Silent, unhappy customers eventually dump you, never to call again. TARP found that for every person who complains, there are 26 who don't. These people can quickly become vigilante customers, those who have made it their mission to besmirch your name whenever the opportunity arises.

ASK FOR FEEDBACK AND YE SHALL RECEIVE

Organizations that practice Customer Plus-Delta value customer feedback. For them, Customer Plus-Delta is more than a series of discrete activities; it's a philosophy extolled by a company's leaders through front-line employees. It's bound by a set of rules that makes many of the tried-and-true standards of market research obsolete.

These are the ten golden rules of Customer Plus-Delta:

1. Believe that customers possess good ideas.
2. Gather customer feedback at every opportunity.
3. Focus on continual improvement.
4. Actively solicit good and bad feedback.
5. Don't spend vast sums of money doing it.
6. Seek real-time feedback.
7. Make it easy for customers to provide their feedback (in person, by e-mail, through Web sites, at conferences).
8. Leverage technology to aid your efforts.
9. Share customer feedback throughout the organization.
10. Use input to make changes—and communicate changes back customers.

WHY CUSTOMER PLUS-DELTA IS VALUABLE

It builds loyal and more profitable customers. Understanding custome faction levels can reveal much about the health of your customer the early 1990s, research by Xerox revealed that the company's *very* customers were six times more likely to repurchase products over one to two years than were merely *satisfied* customers.

It improves the quality of products and services. As described in Chapter 2, customers will only evangelize products and services they love and believe in. Compliments and complaints from current and departing customers create opportunities for improvement.

It deepens emotional bonds. Think about the last time a company asked for your feedback. Can you remember? When it actually happens, you may say to yourself, "Wow. They value my opinion. I appreciate being asked." An on-going relationship and dialogue with customers for understanding their opinions show that you care. Don't assume customers wish to be left alone; if you're not sure, ask for their permission. Like karma, goodwill is returned tenfold.

It saves time and money. Launching new products and services can be expensive, time consuming, and risky. Validating new concepts with customers can mitigate a sizable number of large-scale risks. Before you purchase raw materials, before you finalize manufacturing and delivery processes, before you finalize the sales literature and pitches, ask your existing customers to weigh in with their opinions. Let them spot trouble points, and encourage them to be critical.

You'll add to the buzz that you are a customer-centered company. Your customers will tell their friends, colleagues, and family that you value their feedback.

Positive comments can become part of your marketing. You can document the positive comments you receive and use them as testimonials in your brochures, on your Web site, and in your PR efforts.

YEAH, BUT WHAT DO THEY REALLY THINK?

We're all familiar with customer satisfaction surveys. "Did we meet your needs? Yes or No. What is your perception of our service? Rate us 1 to 5 . . . 'blah blah blah.'" These surveys can provide helpful information about what customers think, but the results can be vague and devoid of specifics.

Similarly in service industries, how many times has a restaurant waiter mechanically asked you, "How is everything today?" You give the perfunctory answer "Fine," without even really thinking about it. This standard question has been asked so many times, without much real interest from the restaurant, that the whole exercise seems a waste of time.

If we really want to know what customers think, we must dig deeper as shown in the following:

- What do current customers say they *love* about you?
- What do they say you should improve, or when's the last time they say you angered them? A waiter asking this question would definitely get a diner's attention!
- What do they value the most about your company?
- What do they say when they recommend you to others?
- Which customers recommend you the most?

Asking these specific questions can lead to deeper insights and improved results.

HOW CUSTOMER FEEDBACK REPOSITIONED AN ENTIRE COMPANY

W/M Displays, a company that creates and manufactures point-of-sale (POS) displays for use in retail stores, understands the benefits of Customer Plus-Delta.

Paul Scriba, president of the 50-year old company, wanted to understand how his customers, who manufacture everything from chewing gum to lawn mowers, perceived his products, so he engaged Sloane Communications to find out. Instead of devising a paper-based, quantitative survey filled with a daunting list of multiple-choice questions to grade dubious levels of satisfaction, Sloane conducted journalistic-style interviews with W/M Display's customers over the telephone.

The interviews revealed that W/M's customers thought the displays were of high quality, and they were impressed with W/M's collaborative and creative approach to solving its retail marketing challenges. By digger deeper than any survey could, however, Sloane discovered stories of value, such as these:

- A display for a major mass merchandiser that increased sales 30 percent
- Product introduction support that helped the product become a sales leader in its category
- Innovative ideas that helped clients sell shelf space and key accounts
- Designs that increased display flexibility and reduced costs by 25 percent

Historically, W/M had positioned itself as a manufacturer of high-quality POS displays, but customer interviews indicated that W/M provided even more. Customers considered the value of W/M's process—studying how consumers purchase, examining store environments, and exploring what individual retailers require and prefer from merchandising programs—as valuable as the results produced.

Sloane worked with W/M to reposition it as a services firm that helps customers increase retail sales. With this new positioning, W/M remodeled its sales process, refined its sales conversations, and created brochures that showcase results—helping differentiate itself from competitors even more. The results? "Our sales are up 25 percent annually," Scriba says. "We have added a third shift to keep up with production."[2]

HOW TO DO YOUR OWN CUSTOMER PLUS-DELTA

It's impossible for this book to prescribe specific tactics for every business and product. What works for a consumer packaged goods company is not necessarily applicable to a law firm focusing on employment law. We have included strategy analyses from our case story companies and others as foundation practices to use as a beginning point for understanding how much customers love you.

1. Make real customer contact. Take at least one customer to breakfast or lunch every week. Ask as many questions as you can think of, letting the customer do all the talking. Sounds easy enough, right? Funny how fast our schedules fill up with company—not customer—meetings. Your customers are more important than anything else that could possibly be going on inside your company.

example | **Flying with Herb**

Well known as the Wild Turkey–drinking, Harley-Davidson–riding, maverick chairman of Southwest Airlines, Herb Kelleher is a thoughtful company leader who regularly listens to what customers have to say. He routinely flies on Southwest's planes as a pseudoflight attendant, handing out peanuts and sitting with customers to hear what they say about Southwest's service.

example | **Who's that billionaire in the cheap seats?**

Mark Cuban, owner of the Dallas Mavericks, attends almost every game—home and away—and sits with fans in the seats, not in a skybox. Sometimes he sits with fans in the $8 seats, talking with them and experiencing the games as they do. His mission is to discover what's working and how he can improve their experience.

2. Scour the Web. Use the latest and greatest search engine to discover what people say about you on fan sites, in the newsgroups, and on e-mail discussion lists. An online search helps you discover—and quickly contend with—any customer vigilantes.

example | **Firms use Web lurkers for customer service**

by Chris Woodyard, *USA TODAY,* February 6, 2002

His name evokes a menacing image.

The Lurker. The Starwood Lurker.

Every workday, the Lurker trolls the Internet. He dips into frequent-traveler electronic bulletin boards to check the postings about his employer, Starwood Hotels & Resorts. He ferrets out comments on any of the big hotel chains that operate under Starwood's corporate umbrella—Westin, Sheraton, St. Regis, or W.

And when he finds them: Zap—he strikes.

He dispatches an e-mail to the sender or posts his own message on the electronic bulletin board. Chat room prowlers such as the Starwood Lurker have become common on the Internet. Hotel and airline representatives are increasingly showing up on travel bulletin boards to answer questions or clear up misunderstandings.

They have to. It's one thing when a customer writes or phones in a complaint to a company. It's quite another when the same customer posts a critical e-mail for all the world to see.

What makes Starwood's Lurker special is that his work is now a full-time job. Offline, his name is William Sanders.

He isn't some college-age technogeek. Sanders describes himself, at 47, as the "old guy on the team" and so uncomfortable with technology that "I can't even complete a conference call." Sanders himself lurks in Austin, Texas, where his official title is specialist in the e-communications department.

He's a relative newcomer to electronic bulletin boards, as is Starwood.

The hotel company, like so many others, has quietly watched for months as frequent travelers write missives about their favorite or least favorite hotels, tips about accumulating frequent-traveler points and the like. The most closely monitored of these boards is FlyerTalk, a feature on InsideFlyer.com, which is visited by many frequent travelers. It's considered a powerhouse in the travel industry, with 300,000 visitors a month who generally stay 15 to 30 minutes. Within the FlyerTalk area are individual bulletin boards for each major airline and hotel chain.

Starwood officials say they saw plenty of opportunities to jump into the online conversation, but were reluctant. They say they didn't want to look like they were muscling in on free speech. But once the company made its first posting in the Starwood area of FlyerTalk's bulletin board December 1, the reaction was surprisingly positive. "Starwood rocks!" wrote a contributor in a post to the site 27 minutes after Starwood announced that it would participate there. "It's nice to have a travel company that actually cares about its customers," chimed in another.

"Within minutes of posting the first message under Starwood Preferred Guest, other people on the board started saying, 'It's pretty good you're helping him out,'" says Klaus Buellesbach, global director of customer service.

Since then, Starwood has joined in conversation "sparingly," preferring instead to try to reach anyone who posts a problem through private e-mail.

Monitoring the site became such a top priority that it was deemed essential to find someone who could handle it full time. In came Sanders, plucked from the relatively obscure ranks of customer complaint responders.

Sanders loves lurking.

Instead of getting chewed out over the phone all day as he did in his former job, Sanders says he now remedies travel headaches of hotel guests in the anonymity of cyberspace. "The people here are more savvy," he says.

Sanders spends most of his workday perusing the messages posted on the Starwood site. He also checks the bulletin boards of about a dozen other hotel chains to check for references to Starwood. He has gotten to know his counterparts at competing hotel chains such as Hilton, which have their own lurkers performing the same task.

Sanders is even making a few online friends among the travelers. One Germany-based traveler messages him about every three weeks to mope about how a particular Sheraton never opened in Malaysia.

David Goldsmith says he didn't stay at Starwood hotels two years ago. But after having had good experiences there, room upgrades and other perks that go with elite frequent-stay status, he says Starwood—and the Lurker—have made him a believer.

And Randy Petersen, the frequent-flier mile expert who runs InsideFlyer, says he thinks the lurkers serve a purpose.

"Customer service is, in theory, about listening and resolving issues with your customers," he says. "In this case, FlyerTalk has become a bit of a surrogate center for that to take place." Sanders is gratified to hear things like that. He sees himself as a fixer.

"It's another way to exceed the expectations of the people who are staying with us," the Lurker says. "That's what it's all about."

3. Gather feedback on your Web site. A page on your organization's web site should *encourage* customers to provide feedback. Make it easy to find the area from anywhere on your site. Collect data for every type of feedback: product complaints, customer service questions, franchising inquiries, and employment questions.

If you want to know what's working well for customers, include an option allowing them to submit their "love" letters, personal stories, and photos of themselves with your product. Feature those stories on your Web site and in your marketing materials. Here's a crazy thought: put your CEO's e-mail address on your Web site.

4. Mine call center data. Be religious about going through call center logs. Some companies receive hundreds of calls every day. That's hundreds of opportunities for customers to express their satisfaction or to make a suggestion. Look for trends. Talk with your call center team often. Listen in on calls every month.

Figure 3.1 | **Create Your Own Plus-Delta**

Ask your audience for feedback in short, bumperstickered encapsulations. Encourage feedback from everyone, especially within groups.

Plus	Delta
What was beneficial?	What can be improved?

5. End every customer meeting with feedback. For anyone who meets with customers in person, use a visual Plus-Delta tool like the one pictured in Figure 3.1. At the conclusion of meetings, ask customers to list what worked well in the meeting; those items go in the Plus column. Then ask customers what could be improved next time; those items go in the Delta column. Tell your participants that the session has no right or wrong answers and that it's not a time for debate. Instead, it's an opportunity for honest, immediate feedback on the service just delivered.

The beauty of the Plus-Delta tool is that it is a five-minute brainstorming session. At your next meeting with the customer, open with how you have addressed the deltas raised at the last meeting. Plus-Delta can work for phone meetings, too.

6. Interview your customers. This is not the same as conducting focus groups. Ask an independent third party to perform in-depth, in-person, or phone interviews to capture what customers really think. Work with customers to understand the value of your products and how they describe your organization's value proposition and product offerings.

7. Use online surveys. Web surveys allow you to get feedback quickly and cost effectively. Mix in a few open-ended questions that help you get a better picture of how your customers feel about you. Try questions such as: "What one thing do you value most about our company?" You'll get amazing answers that you can use in your marketing materials; your ad agency would never have been able to dream up such genuine and insightful copy.

example | A broadcaster listens

Chicago's WBEZ is the third largest public radio station in the country. It has 550,000 listeners and 45,000 members—loyal customers, if you will—who support the station's programming with financial contributions.

A 15-member Listener Advisory Council provides WBEZ feedback on how the station is fulfilling its mission, which is to serve the community. This is no easy task; the Chicagoland area is home to roughly 7 million people. Gathering data is a challenge for a volunteer group with no budget.

Before 2002, the Listener Advisory Council usually conducted in-person surveys using volunteers at events. It was a time-intensive process; data had to be manually entered into a computer for analysis. At one point, the council considered calling listeners at home for feedback, but without a budget to hire a polling firm, many volunteers would be needed. The negatives associated with calling people at home outweighed the benefits.

Finally, a new plan was devised: take advantage of the reach and efficiency of the Internet by using a Web-based survey. In January 2002, the station launched a 12-question survey. Respondents were asked a series of multiple-choice questions about on-air programming and listening habits. Two open-ended questions asked:

- What is the one thing you value the most about Chicago Public Radio?
- If you could suggest one thing Chicago Public Radio could do to improve its service to the community, what would that be?

Sent once to the station's in-house e-mail list, the survey generated more than 800 responses in two weeks. Hundreds of suggestions poured in, from better traffic reporting and additional coverage of local political news to improving the station's fundraising efforts. Responses were informative, constructive, often passionate, and even included some 150-word essays.

Many answers, like the following, were a marketer's dream.

- "[WBEZ] treats me like a person with a brain . . . gives me something to think about, helps me explore the issues of the day."
- "Since listening to [WBEZ], I have become well informed, better educated, and a more aware person. I did not finish college but am able to participate in conversations with the most intelligent people around because of [WBEZ]. People are often amazed that I can discuss politics, the economy, world affairs, etc. Not because they think I am not bright, but because I have knowledge that many people do not."
- "I feel a sense of community with the producers of the programming and the staff at WBEZ and the other listeners. You are my neighborhood. I feel at home whenever WBEZ is on."[3]

Suggested improvements included:

- "The 'Chicago Matters' series on the public schools was absolutely amazing. More programming in that vein would be great."
- "One day a week, maybe Wednesday during AM and PM drives, have an events bulletin board (so there might still be time to plan on going) dealing with museums, music opportunities, festivals, etc."
- "When you have 'experts' on discussing public housing, why not one of us who lives there? More inside information."
- "Traffic reports are usually not timely. By the time they report an accident, it has usually been cleared up."[4]

example | **P&G goes WWW**

Procter & Gamble spends about $150 million annually on consumer research. It used to have a serious addiction to focus groups, with each session costing more than $25,000. In 2001, the consumer products giant decided to break its focus-group dependence and turn to the Internet for feedback; its online tools gather instantaneous consumer feedback about products on the drawing board and current products on store shelves.

In an October 2001 *Wall Street Journal* article, Barbara Lindsey, P&G's director of consumer research services, reported that the company had devoted about half of its research budget to online feedback. Using traditional methods, a simple consumer survey might take three or four weeks and cost as much as $50,000, whereas an Internet survey can be completed in ten days at a cost of $10,000. In effect, P&G discovered that Web-based feedback is five times cheaper and produces data four times faster.

"It can save you a whole lot of time and a whole lot of money," Lindsey says.[5]

8. Create a customer advisory board. Ask your best customers to meet with you, physically or virtually, so they can provide feedback on a regular basis. You'll be surprised at how many of them jump at the chance to be on an advisory board.

example | **When readers write**

In April 2001, washingtonpost.com, the Internet version of the *Washington Post,* invited its readers to join a volunteer advisory panel; over 15,000 people signed up within two months. Thirty-nine percent of the panelists live in the Washington, D.C., area, and 55 percent are spread among 30 different states. The remaining 9 percent of the panelists are scattered among ten different countries.

"The online panel gives us a way to conduct product testing," says Alex Johnston, senior research analyst at Washington-Post.Newsweek Interactive who oversees the readers' group. "With the panel, we get results quicker— in a couple of weeks—compared with previous methods of product testing. We can make changes to existing products faster and react more quickly."[6]

The newspaper has used the panel for many different purposes, including these:

- Product testing for the personalized news product, mywashingtonpost.com: panel feedback has helped the online staff understand the value of existing and new services and how to improve current marketing efforts.
- Testing of new ad formats: washingtonpost.com tests new advertising products for readers' reactions. While many readers typically frown on new advertising, Johnston says his team gathered important insights from the panel.
- Evaluation of special sections: following the events of September 11, the panel was asked to give feedback about the way coverage was presented on the Web site. As a result, site staff had a better understanding of what held the greatest interest for most readers, and designers made adjustments accordingly.

- General perception testing: the panel has participated in an online redesign effort. Surveys ask readers about their connection with various sections, which sections they would like to see more of, and how they would like them to be presented.

* * *

The Internet and advances in technology have made interacting with customers easier and cheaper. Many of the ideas discussed in this chapter rely on the instant nature of the Internet and its ability to connect people in the blink of an idea. Technology allows us to know our customers in ways we never could have before.

Maxine Clark, founder and "chief executive bear" of retailer Build-A-Bear Workshop, says that every company should embrace the instantaneous feedback the Internet delivers. "The Internet has been a huge, huge, positive impact on retailing in general," she says. "Customers expect you to have it as an option for them. And they want it for all kinds of things, whether it's complaining about the business, telling you good things about the business, buying things. People want to give their e-mail address . . . [it's] a way for them to get instant communication and know what is going on."[7]

How organizations act on the free advice of customers differentiates them from competitors. As you'll read in the Build-A-Bear Workshop story (Chapter 13), Maxine Clark has used customer advice to develop 99 percent of her company's products.

Organizations focused on creating customer evangelists exhibit a willingness to share their knowledge with customers, business partners, and their industry. It's a growing phenomenon we call Napsterizing your knowledge.

NAPSTERIZE YOUR KNOWLEDGE

give to receive

"Information wants to be free."[1]

—STEWART BRAND

When 19-year-old programmer and college dropout Shawn Fanning wrote a computer program in 1999 to help his roommate find and share MP3 music files, the program allowed Web surfers to open their hard drives to other people and do the same.

He named his program Napster, a nickname given to him years earlier. In 18 months the world of computing and knowledge sharing changed. Word of Napster spread like an enormous, worldwide fire. Napster quickly became home to a community of 50 million people who shared about 9.4 million files with one another every day.

It didn't take long for the lawyers to get involved; based on a suit brought by the Recording Industry Association of America (RIAA) and a number of record companies, Judge Marilyn Hall Patel of U.S. district court ordered Napster, six months before the company's two-year anniversary, to halt the trading of music files. Backed by the RIAA, the American legal system killed Napster.

The RIAA argued that Napster was stealing millions of dollars from its bank account because consumers were obtaining songs for free instead of paying $17.95 for full-length CDs. Record companies had long wielded an iron hand over how customers used their intellectual property, and Napster wasn't about to change that. Record companies said they controlled standards and distribution; Napster strayed on to its turf, and it deserved to be whacked.

Having one's intellectual property "Napsterized" was suddenly giving other industries fits, namely big media companies. Movie studios, television production companies, and book publishers feared they were next. Once something is digitized, all it needs is a distribution system, and that's what Napster delivered.

The widespread and sometimes irrational fear of getting Napsterized was evident with the appearance of a February 5, 2001, article in the *National Underwriter,* a publication for the insurance and financial services industry. It warned that time was running out for the technologically challenged insurance industry because it shared the same risk factors with the entertainment industry: a highly regulated market, products based on information, a few dominant sellers without real competition, and a large number of customers with no easy way to self-organize. The article argued that Napster-like clones would put the industry on a "hit list" and eventually "shake [the industry] to its roots with an alternative e-business model."[2]

National Underwriter's specious argument had it partly right: Napster-like clones can shake up an industry by providing faster and more efficient models to share and distribute information. The models also make sampling highly efficient; in fact, Napster was the best try-before-you-buy model ever created.

Consider what happened to record sales before, during, and after Napster. In 2000, with the service in full swing, record sales were up 4 percent, according to Soundscan, a company that tracks record sales. After Judge Patel shut Napster down in early 2001, record sales for that year declined 5 percent. In fact, this was the first time in SoundScan's ten-year history that music sales decreased.

Although it's possible that such factors as competition, rising prices, changing demographics, or a lack of anything worth buying could have affected sales, a June 2000 study by Yankelovich Partners confirms Napster's positive effect. The research firm found that among the 16,000 Americans it surveyed, 59 percent who downloaded music said that they later bought the CD.

It seems that Napster stimulated sales because it created bite-size chunks of otherwise expensive CDs. After all, consumer packaged-good companies like P&G and Unilever have successfully made small boxes of soap, laundry detergent, and just about every product found in a box available for years as an inducement to consumers to buy. Why not music? Joel Selvin, the *San Francisco Chronicle's* pop music editor, says that "Napster

encouraged people to try new music they wouldn't necessarily spend money to check out."[3]

THE LESSONS OF NAPSTER

The grassroots, rapid-growth adoption of Napster indicates the makings of a new type of distribution channel and value proposition. Companies that share their intellectual property and business processes with customers and partners increase the perceived and actual value of their products and services. This axiom is proven by SolutionPeople, a creativity and consulting firm. As fully explained in Chapter 10, SolutionPeople makes its knowledge available in a handheld tool and in the way it conducts its creativity workshops. A competitor could conceivably take the company's ideas and processes and copy them, but SolutionPeople has proven since its launch in 1989 that success comes from consistently strong execution.

Companies that Napsterize their knowledge in the marketplace tend to enjoy a marketplace response of help and intellectual capital improvements. For marketers, Napster's rapid growth and influence teach at least five key lessons.

1. Making intellectual property widely available can open avenues for new products and services.
2. The Internet and peer-to-peer technology used in Napster allow information to be shared and passed to others at light speed.
3. The creation of new technology is unending; marketers must continue to adapt and innovate to ride the waves of opportunity that new technologies bring.
4. Customers expect open platforms and try-before-you-buy models.
5. Customers like to join communities to share and exchange data on a one-to-one or one-to-many level.

Napster-like models have the potential to bring about wholesale changes in marketing strategies, company strategies, and perhaps entire industries. Napster-like entrants are good for the marketplace: they prompt industries to reassess their market position and, ultimately, their value to customers.

In the end, Napsterizing has a positive effect; Napsterizing your knowledge widens the information portal to your customers. Napsterization allows stronger ownership of your product or service, thereby making it easier for customers to share with friends and colleagues.

NAPSTERIZED INDUSTRIES

Spurred by the success of Napster-like distribution as well as the open source software movement, individuals and companies in several industries have initiated major plays to disseminate their intellectual capital across multiple channels.

The Software Industry

Web server software is what makes Web sites accessible. The most widely used Web server software is not made by Microsoft, IBM, or Sun. It's Apache, and it's free. In 1995 a group of programmers worked together to fix Rob McCool's popular (yet "buggy") software known as an HTTP (HyperText Transfer Protocol) server. The resulting program was called Apache because it was "A-patchy" server. In 1999, the programmers formed the Apache Software Foundation to provide organizational, legal, and financial support for Apache Server. In 2002, free Apache commanded 58 percent of the Web server market, according to Netshare.

Finnish programmer Linus Torvalds created the Linux operating system in 1991. Several years later, Linux had grown and matured thanks to several thousand volunteer programmers across the world. Linux is now supported by industry giants IBM and Oracle. According to IDC, an information technology (IT) research firm, Linux commanded one-third of the server market in 2001; by 2005, IDC expects Linux to be installed on 41 percent of all computer servers in the world.

The Manufacturing Industry

In March 2001, the Ennex Company of Los Angeles launched a relatively low-cost fabrication machine that uses open-standard digital files to create manufactured products. These digital files can be shared using Napster-like programs and can be modified using existing 3-D programs. For instance, a designer could create a two-dimensional version of a Barbie doll. After loading the file into a 3-D program, the designer can bend, twist, and shape the Barbie doll into an entirely new doll. Once completed, the designer sends the file to a fabricator for production. Call it manufacturing for the masses. By making the development process open and more standardized, Ennex is betting that more companies will take advantage of the cost savings in design to manufacture additional products.[4]

The Education Industry

The Massachusetts Institute of Technology (MIT) is publishing its entire curriculum—lecture notes, assignments, sample problems, reading lists for 500 courses—on the Internet. By 2010, it will have posted the materials for 1,500 additional courses. No passwords. No monthly subscription. Free for everyone. MIT's strategy is to present the value of its intellectual capital as an up-front offering; the university calculates that its return will be smarter high school students who want to attend MIT for the "experience" of interacting with top-notch students and researchers. At the same time, MIT wants to push the frontiers of its knowledge by giving other researchers the chance to increase the universe of knowledge. MIT President Charles M. Vest says the initiative, dubbed MIT Open CourseWare, "expresses our belief in the way education can be advanced—by constantly widening access to information and by inspiring others to participate."[5]

The Publishing Industry

In 2000, author Seth Godin wrote *Unleashing the Ideavirus,* a book whose premise is that an engaging idea can travel through the Internet like a fast-moving virus. To prove his point, he released *Unleashing the Ideavirus* as an e-book on his Web site <www.ideavirus.com>, encouraging readers to download it for free and tell friends about it. A hardcover version was also available, but for $40. One of the book's mottos: "The more you give away, the more it's worth." The results were telling: 400,000 readers downloaded the book in the first 30 days of its release, making it the most read e-book ever. Eventually, the book was downloaded more than 1 million times because friends told friends about Godin's book, and the hardcover version reached number four on Amazon's bestseller list.

Amazon publicly ranks sales of its products, which helps customers understand the relative popularity of the book they are about to purchase. The charts help publishers and authors track a book's popularity by the hour; when a book appears one hour on a nationally syndicated radio program, you can watch the Amazon sales skyrocket the next hour. O'Reilly & Associates, a publisher of technology titles, developed special software to check the Amazon rankings daily and alert O'Reilly to the movement of its titles and those of its competitors.

The Professional Services Industry

Mayer, Brown, Rowe & Maw, the tenth largest law firm in the world, develops and hosts free Web sites that provide information on legal specialties. The firm hosts sites like Securitization.net, a free online resource for information on structured finance. The site helps industry members stay current on global structured finance developments from a growing list of industry participants who regularly provide commentary, news, rating criteria, accounting regulation analyses, legal analyses, and deal descriptions. The site even features content from a competing firm. It does not loudly brandish the Mayer, Brown, Rowe & Maw logo, and only a small link at the bottom of the front page mentions the firm. By spearheading a comprehensive portal, or hub of information, about a specific topic, the law firm subtly positions itself as a leader in the area of structured finance.

As the widespread adoption of the Linux operating system has shown, Napsterizing one's intellectual efforts can help create an industry standard. Napsterized knowledge means wider acceptance of products and services.

BUILD THE BUZZ
spreading the word

"Buzz is not about elegant advertising or glitzy trade shows. It's about what customers—the people who pay for products—tell each other."

—EMANUEL ROSEN, author of *The Anatomy of Buzz*

In the customer evangelism model, buzz is the pathway that helps shepherd new customers into your company's front-row pews. Each wave of buzz provides your evangelists with another reason to extol you. Buzz helps people discover your business faster than do traditional marketing programs. It helps your salespeople develop relationships, because prospects already have some knowledge of your product. In some cases, buzz sells the product by itself.

To understand buzz is to appreciate its influence. Consulting firm McKinsey & Company estimates that 67 percent of the U.S. economy is influenced by buzz. Aside from the industries most associated with buzz, such as entertainment and fashion, McKinsey cites finance, travel, publishing, automotive, pharmaceuticals, and even agriculture as industries that are buzz-worthy.

DEFINING BUZZ

What is buzz, really? Emanuel Rosen, the dean of buzz, wrote the book, literally, on understanding how it works; *The Anatomy of Buzz* dissects the launch points, trajectories, and communication systems that fuel buzz.

Rosen began his quest for buzz knowledge in the late 1990s, when he was in charge of marketing for a Silicon Valley software company that had yet to release its product. Called EndNote, it's a software tool that helps researchers and authors keep track of their references and compile bibliographies for their research papers and books. One day, before the product was even ready, a purchase order arrived from Princeton University in New Jersey.

"It really shocked me," Rosen says. "Suddenly someone from the outside world recognizes it. It's weird. You have this feeling of Wow! It's actually happening."[1] Even though only a handful of people in the world were supposed to know about the product at the time, EndNote had good buzz.

So what is buzz, exactly? Is it different from word of mouth? Word of mouth is "mainly face-to-face communication," Rosen says, when two people share information or opinions with one another.

"Listen, you have to see the movie *A Beautiful Mind* that I saw yesterday. Have you seen it?" he asks, suddenly as we sit with Rosen in his adopted home of Palo Alto, California. "Not yet," we say. "You really have to see it. OK?" For several minutes we discuss the film's attributes, its leading man, Russell Crowe, and Crowe's previous work. We share a moment of connection. "So this is a comment that went from my brain to your brain, and when you add up all the comments that travel among people at a certain point in time about *A Beautiful Mind,* that's the buzz about it," Rosen says.[2]

Buzz includes the multitude of conversations that exist in person and on the Web in chat rooms, bulletin boards, and forwarded e-mails. As Rosen defines it, buzz is "the aggregate of all person-to-person communication about a particular product, service, or company at any point in time."[3] Taking that into account, we say:

Buzz = Word of Mouth + Word of Mouse

Marketers love buzz because it can hurtle a product into the stratosphere of the highly visible. Products like the following that seem to have hit earth like an attention-getting asteroid are a testament to the mystery of buzz.

- Beanie Babies
- Razor Scooters
- Palm handheld organizers

- iPod MP3 player
- *The Blair Witch Project*
- *The Tipping Point: How Little Things Can Make a Big Difference*

HOW BUZZ SPREADS

To become a master buzz marketer, one must understand that buzz travels over invisible networks. Pick up an in-flight magazine and examine the airline's flight paths. Among the paths you'll see hubs, where flights originate and end. Imagine the hubs as people and the flight paths as connections between people. Buzz travels through these connections via face-to-face meetings, the Internet, phone calls, and the like.

Rosen's term for buzz spreaders is *hubs*. Hubs are trusted sources of information who disseminate information quickly. There are two types of hubs.

1. *Megahubs.* Writers at newspapers and magazines; prominent politicians; Oprah
2. *Individual network hubs.* People in the community who can influence a sizable network of coworkers, friends, and family—people in your office who always seem to know the latest movie, fashion, or gadget

HOW BUZZ IS CREATED

Now that we know how buzz spreads, what causes it in the first place?

Some products are "contagious," meaning that people are "infected" with the idea of the product just by seeing it in use by someone else. Products or services with high visibility cause buzz. Personal digital assistants like the Palm Pilot, the Motorola StarTac cell phone, and a number of the early digital cameras were naturally contagious because they were used in public places. It's hard not to engage in a conversation with someone who is using a sleek and sexy titanium Apple iBook laptop computer.

The hit HBO series *The Sopranos* was contagious because it's a brilliantly written show, and it's about people. Colorful and unusual people. Our innate interest in other people prompts us to talk about them, especially if they are Mafia hoods. Buzz about a restaurant is often about the people who eat there. Movie buzz is often focused on the real-life actors in the film.

Taking all that into account, how do you create customer evangelists by tapping in to network hubs?

- Be diligent in finding and tracking network hubs. Join the networking groups that your customers belong to. Find out who the "influencers" in these groups are, and form relationships with them.
- Target the hubs first with a new product or service; network hubs love to be the first to know something new.
- Bring the network hubs to forums where they can talk with others. For example, Apple holds twice yearly customer love fests called MacWorld, where tens of thousands of company enthusiasts are courted by CEO Steve Jobs, renew old friendships, and wax about all things Macintosh.
- Devise ways to make sure others see hubs using your products. For example, PowerBar created a "PowerBar Elite" program. Athletes earn money when their picture appears in the media eating PowerBars or wearing PowerBar gear.

The main lesson here is that individuals, not just the traditional megahubs, can help sell your product. Buzz-based programs that engage everyday influencers can be an addition (or a substitution) to the mass media approach that most PR firms employ.

By talking directly with your customers, finding individual champions, and establishing relationships with the champions, you are on your way to creating good buzz.

THE MYTHS OF BUZZ

A *Harvard Business Review* article sheds light on this phenomenon, which the author calls "explosive self-generating demand." In "The Buzz on Buzz," author Renee Dye explains that before companies can take full advantage of buzz, executives must rid themselves of five common misconceptions about how buzz works, as shown in Figure 5.1.

BUZZ AND PUBLIC RELATIONS

"Ed Rush might have been a great ref, but I wouldn't hire him to manage a Dairy Queen."[4]

—MARK CUBAN, owner of the Dallas Mavericks, accusing the NBA's director of officials of mismanaging the league's officiating

With one comment on January 8, 2002, an outspoken NBA owner launched a media frenzy that lasted several weeks. After a bad call against

Figure 5.1 | **The Five Myths of Buzz**

Myth	Reality
1. Only outrageous or edgy products are buzz worthy.	The most unlikely products, like prescription drugs, can generate tremendous buzz.
2. Buzz just happens.	Buzz is increasingly the result of shrewd marketing tactics in which companies seed a vanguard group, ration supplies, use celebrities to generate buzz, leverage the power of lists, and initiate grassroots marketing.
3. The best buzz starters are your best customers.	Often, a counterculture has a greater ability to start buzz.
4. To profit from buzz, you must act first and fast.	Copycat companies can reap substantial profits if they know when to jump in—and where not to.
5. The media and advertising are needed to create buzz.	When used too early or too much, the media and advertising can squelch buzz before it ignites.

Source: Renee Dye, "The Buzz on Buzz," *Harvard Business Review,* November-December 2000. (Reprinted with permission. © 2000 by the Harvard Business School Publishing Corporation; all rights reserved.)

the Mavericks in a game with San Antonio, Cuban says his comment about not hiring the NBA's officiating chief to manage a Dairy Queen "just came out" during an interview with the *Dallas Morning News*. NBA Commissioner David Stern was not pleased. He slapped Cuban with a $500,000 fine, the highest amount ever levied against an individual in professional sports. (Cuban matched the fine, as he does with all of the other fines he's received from the NBA, with a donation to charity.)

Stern's action generated untold amounts of buzz. Suddenly, fans and sports writers across the country squared off. Some writers called Cuban an overbearing loudmouth. NBA fan sites cheered Cuban for taking on "the system." Amateur NBA fan sites characterized Stern as a "soulless money-grubbing suit." All in all, it was high drama in the NBA, something the league hadn't seen since Michael Jordan's first retirement.

Dairy Queen, proving itself to be as media savvy as Cuban, issued a challenge: perhaps Cuban should try managing a DQ for a day. A conventional professional sports team owner may have profusely apologized and donated money on behalf of DQ's favorite charity to settle the controversy. But Cuban quickly accepted DQ's challenge.

"It wasn't this preprogrammed marketing plan," Cuban says. "Dairy Queen threw out the opportunity and I said, 'Why not have fun with it?' It's just on that checklist of life . . . I'd read from somebody who thought it was a good experience to work behind a service counter. There was a part of me that's always wanted to get a job at McDonald's to work for a couple weeks to get a reality check. When that opportunity came along, it was an opportunity for me to add a reality check to my list. And that's why when I got there, I took it seriously."[5]

The rest is buzz history. Cuban reported for work at a DQ store in Coppell, Texas, on January 16 at 6 AM, ready for training. Hundreds of people lined up to be the first for a Cuban-made Billionaire Blizzard. TV crews converged and helicopters flew overhead. Actor Tom Arnold showed up. Cuban appeared live from the store with *Today* show host Katie Couric saying, "Welcome to Dairy Queen! May I take your order?" It was an *event* driven by buzz. The *Dallas Morning News* later reported that the publicity was worth nearly $5 million in equivalent advertising for the Mavericks and Dairy Queen.

Reflecting on the experience a month after the mayhem had subsided, Cuban gives much of the credit to the company he maligned. "It was good for Dairy Queen—they're the ones that created the opportunity to make it good," Cuban says. "It was good for Paris Chapman, the local DQ guy, 'cause he made it good. It was good for me 'cause it was fun; it was a learning experience. It was good for the Mavs because we sold tickets there. People created a fun energy around it, and it made people realize that's what we sell. If what we're saying all along is about having fun, you gotta do fun things. You can't take yourself too seriously."[6]

What can nonbillionaires learn from this modern media lesson?

- If you believe in something, fear not the controversy. Standing up for a cause that benefits a greater good will probably cause waves. But the waves inspire people to talk.
- If someone issues a challenge to you, take it. Have fun with it, and for God's sake, don't take yourself too seriously.
- Act quickly. *If you see an opportunity to create good buzz, take it.* It can be risky, but in the world of buzz, there are no compliments for caution.
- Be a little outrageous. If you let people see the real you, they feel as if they know you. Just as movie buzz is often about the real-life actors, people love to talk about others who put themselves on stage.

FAUX BUZZ

"You like my car?" a good-looking, Banana Republic–clad, 20-something guy says near his car parked on a downtown street. "It's the new Ford Focus, and it's so money, dude! Here, have a Focus key chain." Customer evangelist? No, he's a hired poseur.

Ford used a staged, Hollywood-style buzz approach in 2001 to launch the Ford Focus. Ford recruited a handful of trendy young adults in several cities to drive a Focus for six months. Their job was to hang out with the car in high-traffic areas and distribute Focus-themed trinkets to anyone who looked twice at the car. "We weren't looking for celebrities. We were looking for the assistants to celebrities, party planners, disk jockeys—the people who really seemed to influence what was cool," says Julie Roehm, Ford's marketing communication manager.[7]

To get Canadian consumers talking about Cheer laundry detergent, Procter & Gamble employed brightly outfitted "shoppers" to stage impromptu fashion shows in supermarkets. A July 2001 *Business Week* article described how the actors also happened to prominently mention that their colorful duds were washed in Cheer.

Creating real customer evangelists through buzz takes work. Paying actors to pretend they are real evangelists is just a form of prostitution and trickery.

An October 2001 *Business 2.0* article on buzz quotes McKinsey & Company principal Renee Dye: "I don't think these more manipulative campaigns will go unnoticed by consumers. They're not stupid. The concept of street teams and other face-to-face initiatives may work for now, but in the long term, I think marketers will have to opt for more subtlety."[8]

EXPERIENTIAL BUZZ

As discussed in Chapter 2, customer evangelism begins with a great product. But often it's how the product is experienced that generates the most buzz. Consider the difference between watching a professional basketball game on TV and watching a game in person. From the television experience, you might tell a friend about the outcome of the game and recount a spectacular play. From being at the game, you might tell a friend about any of these:

- The people in a booth outside the arena getting their heads shaved to resemble the team's star player
- How the announcer sounded like the "Let's get ready to rumble!" guy
- The free T-shirts shot out of air guns into the crowd during game breaks

- The cool, hip-hop music played at the game
- How an entire section of the crowd received a coupon for a free Dairy Queen cone when the opponent's star player was "DQ'ed" (disqualified)
- The stylish team uniforms
- The skimpy cheerleaders' uniforms
- The crazy team owner cheering like a wild man on the sidelines
- The funky band that played a concert immediately after the game

By creating identifiable memory points for customers, an organization creates streams of buzz sources. People tell stories about their experiences with friends, family, and coworkers. The people and events described in the above list represent the experience of attending a Dallas Mavericks basketball game in January 2002. Mark Cuban and his marketing chief, Matt Fitzgerald, say their chief objective for fans is a fun and memorable experience, not just a basketball game.

In *The Experience Economy,* authors Joseph Pine and James Gilmore explain how businesses that orchestrate customer experiences "open up possibilities for extraordinary economic expansion." Companies can avoid the commoditization of their products and services by creating value through memorable experiences. "Every business is a stage, and therefore work is theater," they write.[9] As you'll learn in the Build-A-Bear Workshop case story in Chapter 13, a customer experience can be a creative stage for performance, like the company's assembly line where customers make their own teddy bears and stuffed animals.

But often experiences are created just by interactions with company employees. "In the experience economy, any work observed directly by a customer must be recognized as an act of theatre," the authors say.[10]

The case story companies in this book understand this principle and focus on hiring memorable people. For instance, all Build-A-Bear Workshop employees attend "Bear University," a three-week training course. They learn the "Way of the Bear" and are encouraged to be imaginative and tireless in creating memorable experiences with customers.

MEASURING BUZZ

It may seem that measuring an abstract concept like buzz is like counting stars in the sky: How do you count them? How can we possibly know what people are talking about in private conversations? But with conversations among friends and coworkers increasingly taking place in the digital world of e-mail and Web sites, patterns can be observed and measured. In her *Harvard Business Review* article, Dye says that organizations plugged into buzz networks "can predict the spread of buzz by analyzing how different groups of customers interact and influence one another."[11]

One of the largest online customer groups in the world is Yahoo!, the hugely successful—and huge—portal and search engine, which quantifies interest among its 135 million monthly visitors using a "Buzz Index." (See Figure 5.2.) Every day, Yahoo lists the most popular search terms entered into its search engine. It ranks search subjects with a "buzz score," or the percentage of users searching for a subject on a given day. (The number of searches is multiplied by a constant to make the number easier to read.) For example, on March 23, 2002, pop star Britney Spears held the number one spot with a buzz score of 166, having been on the chart for 283 days in a row.

The Internal Revenue Service was number nine on Yahoo!'s Buzz Index—understandable, given that April 15 was three weeks away. Most entries on the hit list are famous people, which underscores the idea that people are fascinated with, and love to talk about, other people.

Yahoo! is extending its buzz chart idea into a service, working with movie companies to correlate online buzz with real ticket purchases. Tim Sanders, Yahoo!'s chief solutions officer, says the company tracks the number of search requests for a specific movie title during a movie's release and compares it with actual ticket sales. What they've found: A near-identical correlation between the numbers of search requests and a film's box office receipts.

Yahoo! is extending this buzz measurement program to other industries: finance, music, car sales. When it adds U.S. census data to the mix, a company can obtain a much clearer picture of who is talking about them, in effect seeing a clearer picture of its prospective customers.

A key to making online buzz work is what Sanders calls "structure," by which he means a clearly defined message and call to action. In the Internet universe, where the underlying premise is "more is more," Sanders says that Yahoo!'s research shows that small and compact is better than big and expansive for generating new buzz, especially for entertainment products.

"Twenty-seven percent of all people who visit a Web site either watch the video or listen to the audio, which is a very concentrated short message that gets the message across," Sanders says.[12] Carefully choosing the right words that are easy to remember and repeat is important. For creating structured buzz, Sanders suggests a "ten-minute Web site." A Web site visitor knows everything she needs to know in ten minutes and can repeat several key messages easily to other people. Most important, the site asks for her e-mail address, which encourages repeating the key messages or unlocks the door to future content.

Figure 5.2 | **Buzz and Box Office Results**

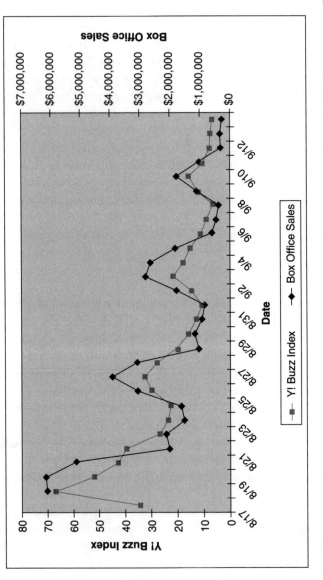

Yahoo! measures buzz as the number of times a person, place, or thing is used as a search term on its site. The company finds that the number of times a specific movie is searched for on its site often correlates with the movie's box office receipts.

Source: Yahoo! Reprinted with permission of Yahoo! Inc. © 2002 by Yahoo! Inc. YAHOO! and the YAHOO! logo are trademarks of YAHOO! Inc.

Here's how to measure buzz-generation programs.

- Always ask new and prospective customers how they discovered you. Ask for the *specific* place, press mention, or person. If the discovery was through a personal referral, what did the referrer say?
- Add a "How did you hear about us?" question to all of your direct marketing activities, such as the sign-up form for your e-mail newsletter or print response cards. If your organization has a call center, have your reps end their calls with this line if the data are not already entered into your customer relationship management system.
- Search the Internet for places where you or your company's name is mentioned.
- Analyze traffic to your Web site. Know which organizations are visiting the most, which part of the world they're in, and which parts of the site they visit most. Most Web site traffic analysis tools can measure search terms entered into search engines that drove visitors to your site.

HOW NICE, SMART MEMES HELP YOU SUCCEED

A meme is a self-explanatory concept that moves through a population like a virus. The word *meme* was coined in 1976 by Oxford biologist Richard Dawkins in his book *The Selfish Gene*. Memes communicate a complete idea simply and compactly.

"Examples of memes are tunes, ideas, catch-phrases, clothes fashions, ways of making pots or of building arches," Dawkins writes. "Just as genes propagate themselves in the gene pool by leaping from body to body via sperms or eggs, so memes propagate themselves in the meme pool by leaping from brain to brain via a process which, in the broad sense, can be called imitation."[13]

Examples of memes from varying industries are Got milk?; America Online; NBC—must see TV; and Intel Inside.

Because it helps people understand what you offer, a meme is more than a tagline. A meme for your company's products and services helps customer evangelists tell your story more succinctly. With a few words neatly arranged in a phrase that rolls off the tongue, a meme will be transmitted from person to person like a handshake.

Which is easier to remember: "We are a marketing consulting firm that helps clients grow their businesses by getting customers to not just buy their products but believe in them so much that they tell everyone they know about them." or "Creating customer evangelists"?

There's no magic formula for creating a meme. It takes a few iterations to get it right. Here are a few helpful hints.

- Understand the real value you provide. Once they experience it, your best customers can articulate the value of your products and services better than you. Ask your customers to describe in their own words how your products help them.
- Keep your meme to a few words. Be simple. A good example is a company named ReachWomen that helps others design marketing campaigns targeted at women.
- Try it out. Try your meme out on lots of people at as many events as possible. When introducing your meme, look for signs of compre-hension or confusion. Listen to how people respond. If they say, "That's just what we need. I should introduce you to our CEO," then your meme works! If the response is, "I'm not sure what you mean," your meme needs work.

CREATE COMMUNITY
bringing customers together

*You are cordially invited to attend our annual reunion to
be held in the Royal York Hotel in downtown
Toronto. The gala event will include dinner,
entertainment, camaraderie, and an examination
of your hernia repair.*

—From an invitation to Shouldice Hospital's annual hernia patient reunion

Each year, a tightly knit group of patients from Shouldice Hospital in Thornhill, Ontario, Canada, get together and party.

They have dinner, entertainment, dancing. Maybe some hula. It's a fun night. Many partygoers have two things in common: They've had hernia surgery, and they are former patients of Shouldice.

Shouldice is not your ordinary hospital. It encourages patients to meet one another and build relationships. Its approach to hospitalization is that it should be an *experience*—a happy and memorable one, not a frightening and forgettable one.

It all began in 1947 when several patients of Dr. Edward Earle Shouldice's suggested that he host a get-together for himself and his patients as a chance to renew friendships and stay in touch. Dr. Shouldice loved the idea, seeing it as the perfect opportunity to launch his idea for annual checkups and for building research data. The first party in 1948 drew 100 patients; since then, the hospital has sponsored annual reunions, with attendance topping 1,500 in the late 1980s, although the reunion has recently been pared back to just under 1,000. A committee of former patients helps the hospital plan the parties.

Shouldice Hospital looks more like a posh country club than a medical facility with its 20 acres of landscaped grounds, a solarium, and a putting green. From the outside, one might not know that inside, 7,500 hernia operations are performed each year; that's more than 30 procedures every day.

The hospital reports a 99 percent success rate with hernia repairs since 1945. It knows because it has painstakingly followed up with every patient—270,000 in all. The hospital contacts 130,000 patients every year by:

- Inviting them to the hospital for checkups
- Hosting the annual reunion of Shouldice alumni (examination included)
- Setting up traveling clinics in small towns around Ontario for those that can't travel to the hospital
- Mailing or e-mailing every single patient a follow-up survey

As Dr. Shouldice envisioned it, the hospital has created a continuous research project that enables it to understand its success rate. It also provides an opportunity to market the success rate.

But hospital officials say it's more than surgical success that lands new patients. Daryl Urquhart, the hospital's marketing director, says Shouldice focuses on creating patient communities. He says that getting to know other people leads to memorable experiences. The following is the hospital's community creation strategy:

- Hospital stays last three to four days. Instead of hectic in-and-out outpatient surgery, patients are encouraged to meet other patients, resulting in a type of "empathetic therapy," an instant support group that compares notes, discusses concerns, and alleviates anxieties about common conditions.
- Each room has two beds so that each patient has a "buddy" during his stay.
- Phones and television sets are located only in communal areas; none are in patient rooms. This small detail helps keep patients out of their beds, walking around, and meeting others.
- Patients eat in a common dining room with tables of six.
- The hospital has billiards, shuffleboard, and a common area for playing cards in addition to the solarium and putting green.

During its 55-year history, Shouldice has often been the talk of Canada's medical establishment. In 2001, a study by Concordia University in Montreal found that of new patients:

- 49 percent were referrals from former patients
- 34 percent were referrals by health care professionals (physicians, chiropractors, dentists, etc.)
- 13 percent were referrals from acquaintances who had heard of Shouldice
- 3 percent were from news articles
- 1 percent were from the Internet

Almost half of all patients heard about Shouldice from former patients, who Urquhart calls "the apostles." "It's our job to make sure that every patient who walks out the door is an apostle and not a terrorist," he says.[1] A terrorist, he explains, is "an unhappy customer who makes it his business to destroy your business." Urquhart says the hospital has a high rate of evangelism because "we focus on not just the surgery but on the entire experience." Much of the experience is a result of the community building among patients and the lifetime follow-up.

WHY COMMUNITY?

Organizations that create customer evangelists often also create customer communities. The communities create a sense of belonging for customers, of being part of something bigger than themselves. An April 2001 *Forbes* article described the passion that Harley-Davidson customers feel about the company as something akin to a "movement that existed before you were born and will continue beyond your finite life span."[2]

Enabling customers to connect with each other and with you provides benefits for all the involved parties. It helps customers get advice on buying things and support for things they've already bought, as well as connect with like-minded people for social reasons. For companies, customer communities build loyalty, provide valuable feedback, and contribute to increased sales. Marketers in our case story companies know this to be true, although they admit the community effect can be hard to measure. For e-commerce Web sites, measuring the effect of online community is easier. A McKinsey-Jupiter Media Metrix study released in 2001 showed that users of Web community features generated two-thirds of sales despite accounting for only one-third of the site's visitors. Users who contributed product reviews or posted messages visited the Web sites nine times more often and remained twice as loyal, buying products nearly twice as often. Users who read but didn't contribute to community interaction were more frequent visitors and buyers.

FAST COMPANY AND THE COMPANY OF FRIENDS

Profiling mavericks and trendsetters, *Fast Company* magazine chronicles new ideas in business and work that are breaking molds and delivering results. True to form, the magazine has been breaking the business-as-usual model in magazine publishing with its Company of Friends (CoF) community. *Fast Company* writer and editor Heath Row launched CoF in 1997 to help readers continue the "conversations" the magazine began in its printed pages. Five years later, the CoF has sprouted into 165 local groups in 35 countries, with 44,000 members.

"We always wanted our stories to start conversations," Row says. "We wanted to get people talking."[3] With no budget to work with, Row offered to connect readers himself into groups using e-mail. By February 1998, his idea had grown into a list of 1,000 names. Like a gangly teenager, Row's idea had a lot of momentum and was outgrowing its original clothes. Now, Web-based software informs subscribers and nonsubscribers alike about upcoming events in their hometown and manages local e-mail discussion lists. An army of volunteers coordinates each locale's efforts.

Row says that Company of Friends members have:

- Started companies together
- Gotten jobs
- Found employees
- Moved to a new city and built a social and professional network in record time
- Obtained book publishing contracts
- Met and gotten married

The events of Sept. 11, 2001, galvanized the importance of CoF to Row and the magazine. "The Company of Friends organized a network of guides for stranded travelers," Row says. "If someone was stuck in the city somewhere because they couldn't get where they were going, Company of Friends members were welcoming them into their homes as hosts, taking them out for dinner, showing them the city, and making their stranded time as fun and comfortable as possible."[4]

The CoF has had a "substantial" influence on the magazine's subscription base of 800,000 during the program's five years, Row says. "People come to the Company of Friends now because of the Company of Friends, often not even knowing about the magazine. People are dragging friends to some workshops saying, 'You have to meet these people. You have to be part of this conversation. You have to hear this speaker.' And then they show up and there's something larger behind it. And so it does introduce people to the magazine."[5]

Here is Row's advice on creating a community.

- Just try it. Proceed in an honest and realistic way. If it's not working, don't hesitate to stop.
- Stay involved. Employee participation nurtures the community, so company bulletin boards ignored by staff are pointless. "If you're not participating, don't bother," Row says.[6]
- Loosen up. CoF has succeeded because of a hands-off approach. Avoid thick binders instructing coordinators how to manage the community. Let groups decide when, where, and why they do what they do. "Innovation happens," Row says. "If we had more control, less creativity would be expressed, and we'd have fewer ideas to share within the network."[7]

THE SHAPE OF CUSTOMER COMMUNITIES

Community works differently for each organization. What's consistently the same, however, is interacting with customers to understand their connection with you and others like themselves.

To bring customers together, companies use in-person events as well as online communities. In fact, combining both methods often maximizes interaction among an organization's various constituencies. A few examples of successful community programs are described in the following sections.

In-Person Events

Saturn, a division of General Motors, hosts approximately 60,000 owners and guests every summer for a two-day extravaganza at Saturn's Spring Hill, Tennessee, manufacturing facility. But it's no ordinary picnic: There are parades, athletic competitions, car club activities, test drives of the latest models, food stations, a carnival fair, opening and closing ceremonies, and live music, including a lively rhythmic interpretation of the history and philosophy of Saturn. The event's primo benefit is the tour of the plant.

Retailers help owners plan caravans to Spring Hill from various points across the United States. Caravans stop at Saturn stores and at interesting attractions along the way, pick up other owners at strategic locations, and make a grand entrance at the Spring Hill Homecoming site. For those who can't make it to Spring Hill, at least 150,000 additional owners participate in Homecoming events at Saturn retail stores across the country.

Clubs

Because Nestlé-owned Buitoni pasta company wants to be more than a pasta maker—its objective being the helpful authority on Italian food—it created the "Casa Buitoni Club" as a community and loyalty program. Its grassroots efforts of in-store sampling and sponsorship of popular sporting events helped build a database of 200,000 customers in two years. These customers were invited to join the club, whose members would receive:

- A full-color quarterly newsletter
- Pasta recipes
- Discount vouchers
- A toll-free number for cooking advice
- A chance to win a visit to the original Casa Buitoni villa in Tuscany
- Information about gourmet cooking weekends
- An opportunity to sample new products

Membership in the club has grown through word of mouth and low-cost channels like public relations events and invitations on the packages of pasta. Buitoni pasta consumption and customer loyalty have been noticeably higher since the club's inception.[8]

User Groups

Harley-Davidson established the Harley Owners Groups (HOGs) in 1983 in response to a growing desire by Harley riders for an organized way to share their passion for ownership. By 1985, 49 local chapters had sprouted around the country with a total membership of 60,000. In 2002, there are 650,000 people in 1,200 chapters worldwide.

Online Bulletin Boards

Dell and Microsoft provide forums on their Web sites for users of the companies' products to help solve each other's technical issues. By sponsoring forums that allow customers to collaborate, the PC maker and software manufacturer save on customer service and support costs.

E-Mail Discussion Groups

Nancy White, president of Full Circle Consulting, created the Online Facilitation e-mail group in August 1999. She leads the group with its 700+ members through discussions of the best practices of online facilitation as well as sharing resources and ideas. White indirectly markets her experience every day by leading and moderating the forum.[9]

E-Mail Newsletters

Weekly or monthly e-mail newsletters help organizations share their latest knowledge of specific topics. O'Reilly & Associates, the technical book publisher, produces 35 newsletters that cover topics from Linux and Java to Perl. There are even special newsletters for librarians, professors, and book retailers. The informative and well-written newsletters deliver real value. Each newsletter has a different editor at the company who includes such information as "Tips for Building Web Database Applications." The O'Reilly model delivers a newsletter of value for a community of subscribers, not one that mindlessly hypes products.

Fan Web Sites

Are there fan sites for your product or service? Embrace them! Extol them for the heroes they are. Add links to fan sites from your Web site. Give Web-based fans special access to pictures and information they can use to build their sites. Send them gift certificates, invitations to special events . . . anything to recognize and reward them for their evangelism.

The worst possible way to deal with fan sites: sending cease and desist letters. In late 2000, Warner Brothers sent letters to hundreds of Harry Potter fan sites, insisting they were infringing on the company's intellectual property rights. The media giant told the teenage Webmasters to take their sites down and, in some cases, demanded they transfer ownership of domain names, such as <www.HarryPotter-world.com>, to Warner Brothers. One angry 15-year-old British fan, Claire Field, took her story to the press, and within days the story made headlines across the country. Two different activist organizations were formed to protest the legal action: PotterWar and Defense Against the Dark Arts (DADA). DADA organized a boycott of all Harry Potter paraphernalia.[10] Companies that send "nastygrams" to fans who build shrines to a company's products and services are themselves nasty.

The right way to work with fan sites: recruit them to help you with marketing. Gordon Paddison, senior vice president of worldwide interactive marketing for New Line Cinema, is responsible for the official *Lord of the Rings* movie Web site. Before building it, he contacted the Webmasters of over 400 fan sites dedicated to J.R.R. Tolkien's literary trilogy.

"I wanted to establish a relationship early on with the influencers, people that I felt would be a conduit for information," Paddison said.[11] The resulting site was filled with screen savers, desktop images, hundreds of still photos, and interviews with the cast and crew. The Paddison strategy is to partner with fan sites and feed them insider tips, thereby inducing them to recruit passionate followers who spread the movie's message.

PUTTING PEOPLE IN YOUR MARKETING

By definition, a community is composed of people. Creating community requires a personal touch. Yes, customers want to know about features, functions, or methodologies of products and services; feature comparisons and product descriptions are a key part of any firm's sales efforts. But prospective customers also want to know about the people side of the equation: Who else has purchased from you? Do they recommend you to others? Who are the people behind your company?

Too often, Web sites, brochures, and ads feature inanimate objects, such as skylines, empty rooms, empty buildings, disconnected body parts, sunsets, sunrises, clocks, watches, glasses, flocks of geese, unintelligible artistic pieces, or just about anything except real-life people. It's marketing to the *Invasion of the Body Snatchers* group.

A customer community helps prospects identify with and connect with other people. Here's how to focus on the people principle in your marketing communications efforts.

- *Dump the stock photography.* Use portraits of customers on your Web site. Chances are that the front page of your Web site is your most visited page, so it's an excellent spot to feature customers. Your featured customers will tell everyone they know about your site.
- *Feature your super-satisfied customers in your advertising.* When you purchase a product or service for the first time, whom do you trust more for advice: an existing customer or the company president/ sales manager? A real customer with a real quote and a real name and title is a potent tool.
- *Make contact information for your key people easily available on your Web site.* Include e-mail addresses for everyone, including senior management.

Don't let senior managers hide from customers and prospects. A key lesson from our case story companies is that key leaders must make themselves accessible to a wide array of customers.

- *Give your business cards a face.* If you're a heavy-duty networker or salesperson, you probably meet dozens of people every month, perhaps every week. Those prospects have a better chance of remembering you when you follow up if they can put a face to a name . . . try putting your picture on your business card. It's not just for real estate agents anymore.
- *Feature portraits and bios of your company people on your Web site.* Let prospects see the personalities behind the corporate curtain. Photos of stern expressions communicate that your company is unfriendly. Smile—it's a portrait, not a police mug shot. Candid photography is better.
- *Develop customer case studies.* Prove how your company has solved customer problems. Feature quotations from customers, not those from your project managers. Then brag about the case studies anywhere and everywhere. Make them a central tool of your salesforce.
- *Humanize your company's e-mail correspondence.* Adopt a more casual conversational style of writing. Correspondence should come from a real person, not "The Management." If you send e-mail, avoid the dreaded "Please do not reply to this e-mail." If companies don't want people to reply to e-mail, they shouldn't send it in the first place.

Business is about people. If you *humanize your marketing,* you're on the road to creating customer evangelists.

* * *

Creating community is key to creating customer evangelists. Community encourages customers to bond with one another underneath the umbrella of your organization's goodwill. One of the strategies to introduce new customers to your community is to offer a specialized, smaller offering, or what we call a "bite-size chunk."

CHAPTER 7

BITE-SIZE CHUNKS
from sampling to evangelism

"Nothing is particularly hard if you divide it into small jobs."[1]

—HENRY FORD

How do you eat a cow? One bite at a time.

That's how companies recruit new customer evangelists, too. Instead of selling customers on the whole kit and "cowboodle" of products, entice them first with a steak dinner. If they love the steak, they'll be back for the rump roast and, later, the whole side of beef.

Break your product and service portfolio into bite-size chunks that are small, easily consumed pieces of what makes your company valuable. For some products, it's samples. For other products, a limited-time or limited-capacity trial version works well. For others, it's a public workshop that provides a service. A "starter" product or service lets customers try your lower-end offerings on their way to purchasing your high-end, more expensive, and complex products.

How does breaking your product into bite-size chunks help create customer evangelists?

- It reduces the risk for decision makers who are purchasing from you for the first time.
- It eliminates inhibitors to the purchase, such as cost or time.
- It gets your great product into customers' hands and minds.

- It shortens the sales cycle and provides a strategic opportunity for customers to experience your products sooner rather than later.
- It spreads buzz by introducing the product or service to more people who can then tell others about it.
- It builds goodwill with customers because it *provides value without requiring a large purchase.*

The last item is key; bite-size chunks provide up-front value. Give to receive. By extending an offer of trust, you implicitly tell customers that you are trustworthy. You're genuine. You are easy to work with. Will some people try and fly? Sure. But your product isn't for everyone every moment of their life. Don't let the potential for a micropercentage of customers taking advantage of your goodwill stop you from offering a bite-size chunk. It's the benefit of reaching all of the other desirable customers you're seeking.

Sampling works well for inexpensive products. Consumer packaged goods companies, like P&G and Unilever, have used this technique for decades by mailing free samples of laundry detergent and shampoo to homes. If you have a great product, half the battle is just getting the customer to try it. Sampling provides the lowest barrier to entry in trying a product. After all, most of us can't resist an offer to try something new . . . and free!

A January 2001 survey by Brand Marketing and the Promotion Marketing Association found that sampling is highly effective for marketers of consumer packaged goods. It asked 1,195 people about their bite-size chunk habits. The following are the results:

- 95 percent have tried a sample.
- 38 percent have tried every sample they have received in the past year.
- 92 percent decided to buy a grocery, household, or health and beauty care product after trying a sample.
- 73 percent became aware of new or improved products through samples.
- 84 percent would consider switching products if they liked the free sample.[2]

The technology industry has had tremendous success using bite-size chunks for creating starter evangelists. Many consumer software companies let prospective customers try a product for a limited time. Customers download free a full-featured version of the software from the company's Web site before it expires after 30 to 90 days or a limited number of uses.

The companies profiled in Chapters 9 through 15 employ varying approaches to their bite-size chunks.

- Krispy Kreme—New customers who have yet to try a Krispy Kreme doughnut are usually handed one in the store. Sometimes clerks include an extra doughnut for customers to munch on while waiting to pay.
- SolutionPeople—This creativity consulting firm for the Fortune 500 charges $60,000 for several days of creative brainstorming, but prospective customers can send a representative to a daylong public session for $850.[3]
- Dallas Mavericks—What's it like to be a season ticket holder for this NBA team? Fans can find out by buying five-game and ten-game packets of tickets. If they like their seats and the overall experience, they can upgrade to a half-season or full-season membership. The team's marketing chief says 55 percent of customers upgrade.[4]
- IBM—Its "Test Drive" program lets programmers test Linux applications online in a simulated IBM environment without having to actually buy IBM hardware.

WebTrendsLive is a Web site traffic monitoring tool from NetIQ. It reports the number of site visitors, what organizations they are visiting from, how they found your Web site, and which pages they view. The company offers customers a limited-feature free version in exchange for placing a WebTrendsLive banner on their Web site.

The free version shows what features are available by upgrading to a paid version. Customers of the free version can evangelize the paid version to others because they understand the benefits, even though they don't use it themselves.

Figure 7.1 illustrates how different companies create bite-size chunks of their products and services.

* * *

As Henry Ford once said, "Nothing is particularly hard if you divide it into small jobs." By dividing your product and service into discrete pieces, you increase exponentially the likelihood of creating new customer evangelists.

Now that customers have tried your product, do they believe in it? Does buying your product contribute to a greater good? Customers believe in causes important to them, and they want to contribute to the success of those causes; if buying your product supports a popular and highly thought of cause, then you are on your way to creating customer evangelists.

Figure 7.1 | A Sampling of Companies' Bite-Size Chunks

Company	Premium Offering / Price	Bite-Size Chunk / Price
Harley-Davison	Motorcycle / $6,000–16,000 retail	Rent a Harley to ride for a day / $120
WebTrendsLive	Software that monitors Web site usage / $35 to $2,000 per month	Limited-use version / free
SolutionPeople	Creativity and innovation training / $60,000 for 3 days	KnowBrainer tool / $75
Faith Popcorn	Keynote speeches / $25,000	Book / $25 retail

CHAPTER 8

CREATE A CAUSE

when business is good

"Evangelism is the process of selling a dream."[1]

—GUY KAWASAKI

Guy Kawasaki and his compatriots at Apple Computer borrowed religion-based evangelism and took it to work.

Apple's secular evangelism launched a new computer that suffered from insufficient software, a lack of storage capacity, a small screen, and a price point higher than its competition. Yet the Mac could compete with lower-priced, richer-featured models made by IBM because Apple was selling a dream, not a computer. Apple sold the Macintosh dream, which was to improve everyone's productivity and creativity. It created an evangelism department and hired marketers to evangelize, evangelize, evangelize.

But to grow, Apple had to convince software vendors to write applications for its operating system. Kawasaki's key competitor—IBM—was a technology stalwart used to setting the standards in the industry; at one point it was even decreed a monopolist. Apple convinced a number of vendors to believe in the Macintosh cause by portraying Big Blue as Big Brother.

To build momentum for its cause, Apple ended up creating what is arguably the most famous television ad in history. Shown only once, during the 1984 Superbowl, Apple's "1984" television commercial famously portrayed Apple's unique, counterculture positioning. Directed by Ridley Scott (who also directed the films *Bladerunner* and *Alien,* among others), the ad portrayed a scowling Orwellian Big Brother figure projected on a giant screen, brainwashing a crowd of glassy-eyed sycophants. Saving the day is a woman sledgehammer thrower whose expert toss destroys the image of Big Brother, allowing everyone to see real light behind the visage.

With the Macintosh, a voiceover promises that "1984 won't be like 1984," George Orwell's classic tale of a world in which "groupthink" is the norm and individualism outlawed. Although the company denied it at the time, Apple's ad pitted itself as David against the IBM Goliath. Nothing less than personal and global freedom was at stake.

"Macintosh started as a vision; then it became a product supported by a cult; finally, it became a cause—propagated by thousands of Macintosh evangelists," says Kawasaki.[2]

That's: vision → product → cult → cause → evangelists

Customer evangelism begins with a great product brought forth from the vision of a leader who has recognized a need in the world. The cult supports the product in its early stages. As the cult or, more appropriately, the customer community grows in size with the support of the organization, the community begins to self-organize around a cause. A good cause is meaningful; it is something to believe in and rally around. Five goals for a company's cause can include:

1. A well-defined vision
2. Making people better
3. Generating big effects
4. Catalyzing selfless actions
5. Polarizing people[3]

A vision is someone's grand plan to change the world—a piece of someone's soul. The vision of Apple founder Steve Jobs was to bring computers to the people—the freethinkers, the creative spirits.

When something helps people become better people, people support it. They tell everyone about the experience; in other words, they become evangelists. This is why self-help books are often best-sellers; sales are fueled by tremendous word of mouth.

Causes can create profound change and affect vast numbers of people. A habitual drunk driver killed Candy Lightner's 13-year-old daughter in 1980. He pleaded guilty but served no jail time; and ten months later, he could legally drive again. An outraged Lightner launched Mothers Against Drunk Driving (MADD). In 2002, MADD's 2 million members in 600 chapters blanketed all 50 states, resulting in considerably tougher drunk-driving laws. Lightner's cause thus had big effects.

Catalyzing, or inspiring, selfless actions is best explained as doing business by the Golden Rule: just do the right thing. For example, after the September 11, 2001, terrorist attacks grounded U.S. airlines, tens of thousands of workers were furloughed or idled. The majority of skycaps' earnings come from tips. During the shutdown of U.S. air travel, Southwest Airlines elected to pay the skycaps what they would have otherwise made, a notably selfless action.

Causes have the power to change society. Conversely, challenges to the status quo can generate fear, uncertainty, and doubt. Highly charged and emotional causes can generate intense passion, pro and con. Abortion and the cause of giving women the right to choose is one example of how polarized people can become. Just watch some of the footage of protesters outside an abortion clinic.

EXAMPLES OF CAUSES

When we think of organizations with causes, we usually think of such nonprofits as the Susan G. Komen Breast Cancer Foundation or the Salvation Army. The cause is the organization's reason for being. Its members wear their values on their sleeves, often literally. People who feel strongly about an issue naturally seek alliances with others who feel the same.

Coauthors Richard Cross and Janet Smith outline how "identity bonds" are formed between customer and company. "Identity bonds are formed when customers admire and identify with values, attitudes, or life-style preferences that they associate with your brand or product," they write in *Customer Bonding: 5 Steps to Lasting Customer Loyalty.* "Customers form an emotional attachment based on their perception of those shared values."[4]

Emotional attachment is key to creating customer evangelists. The two simple ways to build emotional attachment are to (1) adopt a charitable cause (often called cause-related marketing or social-cause marketing) and (2) sell dreams instead of products. Let's look at the differences between these two concepts.

Adopting a Charitable Cause

In 1983, American Express launched a three-month campaign to support refurbishment of the Statue of Liberty. The company donated 1¢ every time a customer used an American Express card and $1 for every new account. The program raised $1.7 million for restoration, and overall American Express card usage rose 28 percent during the campaign's first month; new card applications increased 45 percent.[5]

American Express is credited with coining the term *cause-related marketing*. Business in the Community, a London-based organization focused on corporate social responsibility, defines the term as "a commercial activity by which businesses and charities form a partnership with each other to market an image, product or service for mutual benefit."[6]

Since the advent of American Express's successful campaign, companies have increasingly embraced cause-related marketing. According to the International Events Group, business investing in cause programs jumped more than 400 percent from $125 million in 1990 to $545 million in 1998.

Now more than a short-term tactic to spike sales, cause-related marketing has evolved into a positioning discipline to enhance corporate images with significant bottom-line and community aspects, says Carol Cone, CEO of Cone Communications, a strategic marketing firm that develops and implements cause programs.[7] Her research in the Cone/Roper Cause Related Trends Report has found that American consumers consistently support cause-related programs. The 1999 report found that given a buying choice between two products of equivalent price and quality:

- 78 percent of adults said they'd be more likely to buy a product associated with a cause they care about.
- 66 percent said they'd switch brands to support a cause.
- 61 percent said they'd switch retailers to support a cause.
- 54 percent would pay more for a product that supported a cause they care about.

The Cone/Roper survey found that 80 percent of Americans prefer companies that commit to a specific cause for a long period over those that opt for multiple, short-period causes. Cone calls the former companies "cause branders," that is, companies that take a long-term, stake holder–based approach to integrating social issues into business strategy, brand equity, and organizational identity.[8] Companies that support causes for the long haul win the hearts of customers.

Figure 8.1 outlines companies and their highly visible cause-related marketing efforts.

Selling Dreams instead of Products

In a world of so much stuff, how do you make your product stand out? Sell something bigger than the product itself. Sell a dream. Attract customers by demonstrating that you are in the game for more than meeting

Figure 8.1 | **A Sampling of Companies' Cause-Related Marketing**

Company	Products	Cause(s)
Ben & Jerry's	Ice cream	Support and encourage organizations to eliminate underlying causes of environmental and social problems
The Body Shop	Cosmetics, toiletries	Environmentalism, human rights
Whole Foods	Natural and organic foods	Global organic farming; local food banks; 5 percent of total net profits go to not-for-profit organizations
Wal-Mart	General merchandise	Environment, children, education, community
Avon	Beauty products, jewelry	Women's health, including breast cancer awareness

Source: Company Web sites

your quarterly sales numbers. Evangelize how you are helping your customers live better lives.

This doesn't mean slapping a dreamy slogan on a product and announcing that it will change your customer's life forever. Plenty of late-night TV infomercials already sell nightmares, and customers are skeptical of contrived playacting marketing.

Marrying a product to a cause is not something the marketing department dreams up. A cause helps customers and, most important, embodies the principles and values of an organization's leaders and employees. From the receptionist to the CEO, all company employees show that they believe in the cause with their actions every day. The marketing department communicates the cause's message on the Web, in brochures, through its PR, and in advertising. Figure 8.2 outlines companies selling more than just products.

The idea of cause-driven companies cannot be underestimated, no matter the product. Let's take two well-known companies and explore how they *could* rally customers around a cause. (*Note:* these are suggestions for causes, not actual programs they have undertaken.) The two companies are Coca-Cola, maker of one of the best-known products in the world, and Oral B, a manufacturer of toothbrushes and other dental products.

We then asked two well-known and respected cause-creation experts how the unlikeliest candidates for a company cause—consumer products—could build support for their products. Dan Pallotta is founder and chief executive of Pallotta TeamWorks, an event-marketing firm based in Los

Figure 8.2 | **A Sampling of Companies That Sell More Than Products**

Company	Products	Cause(s)
Apple	Macintosh personal computer	The "democratization of the desktop," whereby previously expensive and exclusive programs and processes are affordable and easier to use
Southwest Airlines	Air transportation	Freedom to connect with loved ones (because of consistently lower airfares)
Starbucks	Coffee	A meeting point for neighborhoods and communities
Dallas Mavericks	Professional basketball	Creating emotional memories
Fast Company	Magazine subscriptions	Showcases the companies and individuals who are inventing the future and reinventing business

Angeles, California. Brian Erwin is vice president of sales and marketing for DigitalMed, a Boulder, Colorado, firm that specializes in e-learning for the health care industry. He is the former head of marketing for O'Reilly & Associates and the former director of activism for the Sierra Club.

How can Coke create a cause? Dan Pallotta says Coca-Cola should "do something really, really radical" if it wants to differentiate itself from Pepsi. "They've got what, $700 million in advertising dollars this year? Here's what we're going to recommend: spend the whole $700 million on a campaign about recycling your Coke cans. Don't talk about the flavor; you got that. People love you. Now make a difference in the world and people will really love you."[9]

How can Oral B, the toothbrush maker, create a cause? Brian Erwin says it's tough but possible. "Maybe I'm not loyal to the toothbrush itself, even though it's a fine toothbrush. But a good corporate entity that does good things in the world will engineer my loyalty, and that will have a positive impact on its brand. If given the choice in the drugstore, I would be inclined to pick that brand. There is an important element of how a company acts as a corporate entity."[10]

MAKING IT EASY

Creating a cause is easy. Getting people to join your cause is hard. Television ads are broadcast. Brochures are delivered. The Web site is up.

Customers discover your company, your product, and your cause, and they want more information. They are considering joining your cause. Now is the moment of truth.

Can people actually join your cause? A simple question, but it can be a serious problem if you can't capitalize on the interest and excitement you've generated. Customers will get frustrated and lose interest if the process isn't smooth.

In *Selling the Dream*, Kawasaki illustrated the complexities of joining a cause. As an experiment in July 1990, his researcher called eight organizations to inquire about signing up. Following are the results:

- Apple, NeXT, and IBM: The researcher asked these computer manufacturers how to join their developer's program in order to write software for their computers.
- Handgun Control, Inc., and the National Rifle Association: The researcher asked for information on membership and volunteer opportunities.
- National Audubon Society, Planned Parenthood, and the Sierra Club: The researcher asked for instructions on joining their causes.

The results were almost comical. Three out of eight organizations never sent materials; and a corporate operator for one of the companies had no idea what her organization's cause was even about.

How have things improved for these same organizations 12 years later? On February 17, 2002, we decided to find out. We used the same methodology but substituted Microsoft for NeXT (which was bought and folded into Apple in December 1996).

In 1990, the World Wide Web didn't exist, so Kawasaki's researcher requested information via telephone; in 2001, all of the organizations had a Web site. Certainly, after having been taken to school by Kawasaki 12 years before, these companies had made *joining* their causes easy, right? Not necessarily.

Apple

<www.apple.com>

A front-page link for "Developer" took us to the Apple Developer Connection (ADC) area, which featured information on every level of the ADC program. We clicked on the very prominent "Join now" button and signed up for the program's lowest level. Signing up online was easy, free, and painless, but the form was several pages long. Although the site promised one, we did not receive a confirmation e-mail but did begin receiving weekly ADC e-mail newsletters.

Result: Joining was easy.

IBM

<www.ibm.com>

IBM's front-page link for "Developers" took us to pages with bountiful amounts of information on products and technologies, but there was no information on how to join its developer program or whether a developer program existed. We signed up for something called the developerWorks e-mail newsletter. A feedback button on the page clicked through to a feedback form, and we asked how to join IBM's developer program. Two days later, an e-mail from Jeannette arrived informing us developerWorks was a content site and that we should join PartnerWorld for Developers. Jeannette included a link, which took us to a Web page to sign up as a "commercial member." After filling out and submitting a very long form, we received a confirmation e-mail in minutes.

Result: Joined, but process was confusing.

Microsoft

<www.microsoft.com>

A "Developer" link on the front page of its site took us to the Microsoft Developer Network (MSDN) page, but it wasn't clear how to join the program. There was lots of information on products and technologies, downloads, training, and events. We decided to just sign up for the free newsletter, but this required a Passport account, too. Four pages later, we had signed up for the Passport account. A confirmation e-mail arrived a few minutes later. We've been receiving MSDN e-mails every two weeks.

Result: Couldn't find anything but the e-mail newsletter list to join.

Handgun Control, Inc.

<www.bradycampaign.org>

Finding this site required research. On June 14, 2001, Handgun Control changed its name to the Brady Campaign to Prevent Gun Violence. The word *join* was nowhere on the front page of the site, but a button for

"Activists" took us to a page that encouraged us to "Become an Activist." We were then presented with the following choices:

- Join the B.E.A.R.
- Write your member of Congress.
- Write to your local newspaper.
- Start Campus Alliance at your school.
- Join our Hechinger Speakers Bureau.
- Give online.

Not knowing what "B.E.A.R" was, it seemed that "join" would take us in the right direction. Clicking the button took us to the "Brady E-Action Response Network." After filling out and submitting the online form, we got an error page.

Note: We gave the Brady Campaign another try a few months later. After completing and submitting the online form, we received a confirmation e-mail in minutes. The Web site's navigation was slightly improved.

Result: Couldn't join on the first try. Successful on second attempt.

National Rifle Association (NRA)

<www.nra.org>

A button named "Join/Renew" on the site's front page took us to another page, where we had to click again on "Join NRA." Very little information could be found on the benefits of membership except that $3.75 of membership dues is designated for a subscription to the organization's magazine. We filled out the form, including our credit card information for the $10 fee. A confirmation e-mail arrived in minutes.

Result: Joined, but unsure of the benefits.

National Audubon Society

<www.audubon.org>

A button named "Join & Support" on the site's front page took us to a page that clearly explained membership benefits. We clicked on the "Join now" button but received an error page.

Note: We tried the National Audubon Society a few months later. This time we were able to fill out the membership form and join at a cost of $20. No confirmation e-mail was received.

Result: Couldn't join at first. Successful on second attempt.

Planned Parenthood

<www.plannedparenthood.org>

A button named "Get Involved" on the front page of the Web site took us to a very busy page that listed many of the following actions to take next:

- Speak out to save *Roe v. Wade.*
- Send a Message of Thanks to Colin Powell for his Support of Condom Use.
- Sign the Petition for Choice!
- Sign the Petition Opposing the Nomination of Judge Pickering.
- Don't De-fund International Family Planning.
- Don't Relegate Women to a Second-Class Status!
- Demand Funding for Comprehensive Sexuality Education.
- Support Contraceptive Equity Legislation.

It was unclear how to simply join Planned Parenthood's cause. A button invited us to join the "Responsible Choices Action Network" from where we could send e-mails and faxes to every member of Congress on issues relating to family planning, sexuality education, and reproductive health. The network, according to the site, would send us e-mail regarding legislation and how to take action. After submitting a form to register for the Responsible Choices Action Network, we did not receive a confirmation e-mail. Several days later, however, the action network sent an e-mail urging us to oppose the nomination of Charles F. Pickering, Sr., to the U.S. Court of Appeals for the Fifth Circuit by replying to the e-mail. (We didn't.) We've been receiving about two e-mails every week since we signed up.

Result: Not sure if we joined Planned Parenthood or just an e-mail list.

Sierra Club

<www.sierraclub.org>

A button named "Join or Give" on the site's front page took us to a page with detailed explanations of membership benefits, including how membership money is used. We clicked the "Join online now" button, filled out the form with our credit card information, and received a confirmation page. It cost $25 to join at the lowest level, but we did not receive an e-mail confirmation of our transaction. We received *Sierra* magazine two weeks later and a Sierra Club backpack a few weeks after that.

Result: Easy to join.

The World Wide Web has certainly improved the ability to get information quickly. Because each organization had a Web site, we could obtain more than what Kawasaki's researcher could 12 years earlier. Actually joining the causes was sometimes complex and a few times impossible. Technology is only great when it works.

Rallying supporters to join your cause is like dating: once they're ready to commit, don't jilt them at the altar.

* * * *

With the six tenets of customer evangelism as guiding principles, we can understand the success of companies loved by their customers. As you'll discover in the chapters ahead, customer evangelism is possible in all types of companies.

Besides an embrace of customer evangelism tenets, we found these additional corollaries.

- *A visible leader.* The willingness of the company founder, chief executive, or senior leader to be out there was key. It often means someone who speaks his mind and does not duck from controversy within his industry. Note: This is different than the charismatic CEO who leads totally by personality rather than leading by example. Employees and customers want company presidents to be *accessible.*
- *A recurring insistence on "doing the right thing."* This consistently applies to customers, employees, and business partners. Companies with legions of customer evangelists recognize that profit is a byproduct of evangelism, not its central purpose.
- *A rather theatrical approach to business.* It seems that good business means good theater. The May Department Store Company's chairman Stanley Goodman used to say: "When customers have fun, they spend more money."[11]
- *An intolerance for being "cheap."* This is not the same as being cost-conscious.
- *A maniacal focus on customer satisfaction.* We found that whereas shareholder value is important, it does not necessarily reside at the top of the company's objectives. Increasing customer value does.

HOT MARKETING NOW
krispy kreme doughnuts

"There's so much word-of-mouth sharing, where someone is
telling someone else about us—our customers feel
like they're helping get the word out because we
don't advertise." [1]

—STAN PARKER, senior vice president for marketing at Krispy Kreme Doughnuts

On December 4, 2001, Darrin Dredge and his friends set up camp at 6:30 pm on a dark but pleasant Kansas night.

A three-quarter moon would be rising in about three hours in the southern sky. Being smart campers, Dredge and his crew brought blankets, board games, food, water, and the latest camping accessories—a portable TV and VCR—to pass the time. As the hours slowly ticked by, others arrived and joined the campsite. Within a few hours, the crowd had swelled to 75 people, some of them prepared for the elements, some not. The night air was filled with the sweet aroma of cooked flour and sugar cane, and hunger pangs stirred in the campers.

But these campers weren't enjoying the night air to escape the bustling life of blue-collar Wichita, which produces more general aviation aircraft than any other city in the world. Darrin Dredge was there to eat the very first confectionary wonder produced by Winston–Salem, North Carolina–based Krispy Kreme Doughnuts. Eleven hours later he would.

Precisely at 5:30 AM, the doors to the store were unlocked. Hundreds of people crowded into the lobby and onto the front lawn. A line of hungry onlookers snaked around the building and down the street, lured by the buzz of Krispy Kreme. Local television, radio, and newspaper reporters swarmed the scene, trying to grasp the magnitude and allure of hot doughnuts bathed in sugary glaze. A maze of cars snarled traffic on East Central. "We love Krispy Kreme doughnuts,"[2] is how Dredge explained the phenomenon.

The scene that morning in Wichita, Kansas, is a familiar one for the executives of Krispy Kreme Doughnuts. In Fresno, California, a reporter described the store opening there as "marked by the kind of hoopla usually reserved for . . . a presidential visit."[3]

Two students from Stuttgart, Germany, saw a story on the Internet that a Krispy Kreme was opening soon in Colorado. They bought $400 plane tickets, skipped school, and flew to Denver a few days later to join the store's opening festivities.[4]

In Issaquah, Washington, a suburb of Seattle, a training location for future Krispy Kreme employees is kept secret for fear that fans will show up at the door begging for doughnuts. Issaquah's mayor is hounded every day about the future opening of a local store. She is astonished by what she calls the company's "cult following."[5] Store openings in Chicago, Buffalo,

Figure 9.1 | **Krispy Kreme**

Another Krispy Kreme store opening, another long, snaking line. Hundreds of customers waited for hours in anticipation of the company's San Diego store opening on December 19, 2000.

Mississauga, Ontario, and a dozen other locales have produced similar stories, especially traffic jams on nearby roadways.

The arrival of a new Krispy Kreme store is an *event*. Years spent cultivating customer goodwill, exploiting buzz opportunities, building friendly, down-home relationships with the media, a go-slow growth plan, and a focus on bygone eras have paid off for Krispy Kreme. It has developed tidal waves of customer evangelism for a product with 11 grams of fat and 200 calories.

Indeed, life is sweet at Krispy Kreme. In its fiscal 2002 year, the company's $394 million in sales topped the previous year's $300 million, an improvement of 31 percent. Even though the company is growing, it's not at the expense of profits; fiscal 2002 profits were $26 million, nearly doubling the previous year's income of $14 million. Weekly per-store sales have risen as fast as the airy dough in the company's products, going from $40,000 in 1996 to nearly $70,000 in 2001 in company-owned stores. (In franchised stores, weekly sales went from $23,000 in 1996 to $41,000 in 2001.)

Each Krispy Kreme location typically rings up $2.5 million each year compared with the $600,000 from each store of rival Dunkin Donuts.[6] Compared to Dunkin' Donuts' 5,200 U.S. stores, Krispy Kreme's 215 in 2002 look puny. But no one is camping outside a new Dunkin' Donuts and calling its customer base a cult either.

Krispy Kreme Doughnuts creates customer evangelists because:

- It starts with a hot product.
- It's not just fried dough; it's an experience.
- Customer communications drive product development.
- The company's roots are in grassroots marketing.
- It gives away doughnuts so that people will buy them.

STARTING WITH A HOT PRODUCT

The doughnut is as old as America. The French have beignets; the Polish paczki has been a berry-filled pastry for hundreds of years. The Dutch who emigrated to New York in the 1600s brought olykoecks, or oily cakes, pastries that were fried in fat.[7] Apparently, even the ancient Romans had their type of fried pastry.

But the modern-day doughnut, the wheel-shaped cake with a hole punched in the middle, is an American invention. There are two theories explaining the doughnut hole. The first is that Pennsylvania Dutch immigrants in the 1800s punched holes in their olykoecks to make them easier to dunk in coffee.[8] The other is that a Maine teenager named Hanson Crockett Gregory punched a hole in a "greasy sinker" because his mother's fried cakes were too soggy in the middle. Evidence of who first punched a hole in an oily cake is inconclusive.

In 1933, French chef Jon LeBeau sold his Paducah, Kentucky, doughnut shop, its secret recipe for yeast-raised doughnuts, and the name *Krispy Kreme* to Vernon Carver Rudolph and a partner, who moved to Nashville to become a doughnut wholesaler, selling to local grocery stores. It wasn't long until Rudolph and his partner had a falling out; Rudolph and two new partners set off in a 1936 Pontiac and arrived in Winston-Salem, North Carolina, with $25 in cash, a few pieces of doughnut-making equipment, the secret recipe, and the Krispy Kreme name. Their plan was to become a wholesaler.

With the smell of fresh doughnuts wafting over the neighborhood, nearby residents soon started knocking on the plant's door, asking to buy a dozen for themselves. Rudolph knocked out a hole in the wall and sold directly to customers through a window. News of the doughnuts spread quickly by word of mouth, and Krispy Kreme became a bustling business, largely confined to the U.S. Southeast.

A year after Rudolph died in 1973, Beatrice Foods bought Krispy Kreme as a wholly owned subsidiary. For six years, Beatrice tried to make Krispy Kreme a fast-food convenience store selling Beatrice-made cookies, sandwiches, soups, and biscuits. "None of it seemed to work," says Stan Parker, Krispy Kreme's marketing chief, who has been with the company since 1997.[9] Beatrice responded by cutting corners, including the use of cheaper ingredients in the secret doughnut mix. In 1980, a group of franchisees borrowed $23 million and bought Krispy Kreme back from Beatrice. Led by Joe McAleer, Sr., the newly independent Krispy Kreme dumped all of the Beatrice products and went back to what it knew best: a love of doughnuts with the original ingredients restored.

It was a good thing that Krispy Kreme was bought from Beatrice, because Americans love doughnuts. Since 1994, doughnut sales in the ever expanding American waistline have been on a roll: from $6.5 billion annually to $9 billion in 2002, according to consulting group Business Trend Analysts. In dollars to doughnuts, that's 10 billion doughnuts and 2.2 trillion calories each year, says the National Restaurant Association.

Krispy Kreme's sugary confections have certainly been a contributing factor to that dual growth. Fresh off the production line, a Krispy Kreme doughnut practically floats. Its sticky glaze glistens brightly. A Krispy Kreme fan on the Internet described it as "like the feeling you have just before you go to sleep, but in the form of a doughnut."

The sleepy Winston-Salem brigade went from southern delicacy to breakout star in 1997, when it opened a store in the media capital of the world—New York City. With someone like Willard Scott on the *Today* show announcing that he worships in "the church of Krispy Kreme," who needs advertising?

Soon, the hungry press discovered the southern charm of the Krispy Kreme mystique and its passionate customer evangelists; dozens upon dozens of stories ensued. "New York was very successful," Parker says in his native North Carolina drawl in an understatement. "I think for the first time there was a realization that this could be a national brand."[10] The media coverage fueled a sugarcoated fire that turned the company into an undiscovered hot prospect.

"We'll be 65 years old this summer [in 2002]," Parker says. "But it's almost like we're a start-up with 65 years of experience."[11]

Lessons learned:

- Customers can only evangelize a good product.
- Trust your hot product—it creates word of mouth.
- Location still matters in retailing.
- When the media come calling, direct them toward your customers to fuel the fire of their evangelism.

AN EXPERIENCE, NOT JUST FRIED DOUGH

Vernon Rudolph loved automation. Because he began his business as a wholesaler for grocery stores, the faster he could produce doughnuts, the more successful he was, so after World War II, Rudolph increased his reliance on automation. Fifty years later, doughnut automation has become *doughnut theater*, a term developed by customers to explain the entertainment value of watching the gleaming and stainless steel doughnut-making machinery. "Each one of our stores is really a small factory," Parker says.[12]

Because the doughnut-making machine requires minimal human intervention, it can also be described as mechanized theater. It's about as wide and long as a semitrailer truck. Using an overhead winch, employees fill the machine's giant vats with the secret recipe batter. An automatic extruder creates a row of four doughnuts; a blast of air creates each doughnut hole. Each row of newborn doughnuts rides its own car up and down a 12-foot tall elevator shaft called a "proofer" for roughly 15 minutes. The heat and humidity in the proofer cause the yeast in each doughnut to rise.

After proofing, the doughnuts inch along in slow motion along a waist-high conveyor belt for several minutes until they are plopped like lemmings into a waiting pond of hot oil. They'll cook for exactly one minute before entering a tiny garage where they are flipped over—four at a time—to cook for exactly one minute more.

A store employee hovers nearby, plucking out misshapen or oddball creations. Like participants in a parade, the doughnuts travel down another conveyor belt before they're drenched in a three-foot wide glazing waterfall. Moments later, an employee carefully scoops up still hot doughnuts from the moving assembly line and drops them into a box. It's all done behind floor-to-ceiling glass with unobstructed views, just like a modern zoo.

Spend an afternoon at the Mountain View, California, store in what's popularly known as Silicon Valley, and you'll see a cross section of America: Asian, Hispanic, East Indian, Anglo, the elderly, the very young, and all the computer programmers in between. Almost everyone spends at least several minutes with faces pressed against the glass, comprehending an assembly line that produces about 3,000 doughnuts an hour. Across the Krispy Kreme nation, that's 5 million doughnuts a day, 2 billion a year.

It took decades before Krispy Kreme realized that putting the doughnut machine on stage was good marketing; until the 1980s, customers had to peer through a small portal to watch the action like a peep show.

Just as Maxine Clark, the founder of fast-growing Build-A-Bear Workshops discovered (Chapter 13), retail customers love in-store "factories." Being somehow involved in the process creates a memorable experience and waves of buzz.

To extend the "stage" experience beyond its permanent locations, Krispy Kreme created a 53-foot store on wheels. In 2002, it began a tour that would wear out even the most veteran touring musical act: 240 days on the road a year with a staff of 10 to 20 for feeding the doughnut hungry at state fairs and festivals in far-flung locations or wherever else Krispy Kreme had not yet caused a stir, Parker says. Fully assembled, the mobile store is a colorful and brightly lit diner that wouldn't be out of place at a state fair. A tall "Hot Doughnuts Now" sign rises high into the sky, complete with colorful lights.

"With some of these heartfelt letters and e-mails we get, we may just surprise somebody one day and show up in their town, like a random act of kindness," Parker says. "A very large random act of kindness."[13]

Just like a permanent store, the touring doughnut mobile is visible doughnut theater. It's buzz on wheels.

Lessons learned:

- Building an experience around a product gets customers involved and connected.
- Continually strive to understand the emotional connections customers feel toward your products and the company.

ENCOURAGING CUSTOMER COMMUNICATIONS DRIVES PRODUCT DEVELOPMENT

Customers drove the concept of doughnut theater. In the 1980s, Joe McAleer and his team listened to the company's customer evangelists and redesigned the stores to make the factory process more accessible. They also complied with requests for drive-through windows, more seating, and a contemporary décor.

It took 40 years for the company to realize that a "Hot Doughnuts Now" sign would be a hot marketing idea. Customers complained they didn't know when hot and fresh doughnuts were available. A franchise owner in Chattanooga, Tennessee, listened to his customers in the 1970s. He bought a window shade and had "Hot Doughnuts Now" printed on it; when the doughnuts were hot, he pulled the window shade down.

Company officials loved the idea. Instead of window shades, Krispy Kreme produced the distinctive green and red neon signs seen today in all of its stores. When the neon's lit, the doughnuts are hot.

"It's one of those great things that a company has to be around long enough to have," CEO Scott Livengood says. "It's the essence of great marketing: This was a manager in one of our stores who listened to our customers."[14]

It's no coincidence that "Hot Doughnuts Now" is the perfect marketing meme. It describes a process and an opportunity. It's also Krispy Kreme's key—and solitary—form of advertising.

It also began a period of transformation for Krispy Kreme from a mostly wholesale business to a mostly consumer business, Parker says. On the wholesale side, the Kroger grocery chain accounts for 10 percent of sales.

Krispy Kreme has expertly tapped into the love customers express freely for its products. The company encourages letters and e-mail to understand how it's doing. Customers write, all right: 6,000 e-mails a month, Parker says. Many customers recount their first experience with a Krispy Kreme.

"Customers send us pictures of themselves eating their first doughnut and how it was a 'little piece of heaven,'" Parker says. "But just as many of them, if not more, talk about the experience. They talk about how it was where their mom and dad took them after church on Sunday. Or the doughnuts they sold for their class's field trip. Or they went there for dates on Saturday night. There's a lot of sharing that happens."[15]

A commercial airline pilot wrote that when he announced that he had bought Krispy Kremes for everyone on his flight from San Diego to Seattle one night, the passengers gasped and broke into applause. "Never in my 17 years of flying for this company . . . have I experienced a more appreciative and happier group of people," the doughnut-eating pilot wrote.[16]

Parker says every customer receives a personal response. "It's about cultivating a relationship with customers," he says. "We always respond to folks, and we don't do it with an autoresponder."[17] From its customer communications research and studies, the company knows that the majority of customers buy more than a dozen doughnuts on average to "take somewhere and share."

"That's a big part of the Krispy Kreme experience. The strength of the Krispy Kreme brand is that our customers have made it strong," Livengood says. "It's not been through advertising campaigns or contrived marketing or our going out to create an image. The brand is what customers have made it."[18]

Through formal and informal research of its own to understand the phenomenon it has created, Parker says it all comes down to two things. "It starts with *an experience*—a hot doughnut—and it elevates pretty quickly into *an emotional connection*. "The more we dug, the more we understood the emotional connection. There wasn't a blueprint in 1995 that would have predicted what's going on today."[19]

Lessons learned:

- Customer ideas can have the biggest impact, even if it takes 40 years to realize.
- Encourage customers to write and describe what your company and its products mean to them.
- When customers take the time to write, take the time to respond with a personalized note.

COMPANY'S ROOTS ARE IN GRASSROOTS MARKETING

Since the 1950s, Krispy Kreme has helped tens of thousands of charitable organizations raise money. In 2001, the company helped raise $27 million for causes in the cities where its stores are located; the year before, it was $19 million. The causes can be everything from church groups and Boy or Girl Scout troops to school band trips, just so long as it's local and nonprofit. "It's a little bit of a business for us, but not much," Parker says. "Our approach is very local."

The ingredients making up Krispy Kreme's grassroots marketing formula are simple yet highly potent.

- Support local charitable organizations by selling them doughnuts at half price.
- Allow the nonprofits to resell the product at full retail price or higher.

- Let the nonprofits keep the profits.
- Get millions of doughnuts into the mouths of people who may never have tried one before.

The roots of Krispy Kreme's grassroots marketing are in avoiding big ad budgets. Low or no budgets help companies think creatively about their marketing tactics, Parker contends. "It's been a way for us to connect with people on a local, grassroots level," he says. "We had to find ways like that."[20]

From all indications, it appears this strategy is key to Krispy Kreme's appeal. Yet from the day the company went public in April 2000, Wall Street analysts pop up like underground gophers every few months and insist that Krispy Kreme start advertising.

Although Parker maintains that customers say they would be disappointed if Krispy Kreme ads started showing up on TV, he won't rule it out.

"We are a public company, and we will advertise if it makes sense," he says. In the meantime, the company's legions of evangelists take care of advertising for the company.

"There's so much word-of-mouth sharing, where someone is telling someone else about us—our customers feel like they're helping get the word out because we don't advertise," Parker says.[21] "It's not uncommon when we open a store—and it's 5:30 AM with a line two to three hours long—that many of the people there have already experienced Krispy Kreme and are bringing their friends and neighbors to the store who haven't experienced it before. They just take it upon themselves to bring the uninitiated down and make sure they get a hot doughnut.

"It would be hard to achieve that in a traditional ad."[22]

Lessons learned:

- Enlist the aid of nonprofit or charitable groups to help sell your product by giving them a wholesale price.
- Conducted well, grassroots marketing creates company ownership among customers.
- In deciding between the advice of customers and the advice of Wall Street analysts, who do you think carries more weight?

GIVING AWAY DOUGHNUTS SO THAT PEOPLE WILL BUY THEM

Outsiders who study Krispy Kreme's marketing strategy are usually surprised to discover the company doesn't follow the traditional four Ps of marketing (product, place, price, and promotion). That's been the experience of Karen Mishra's marketing students at Wake Forest University in Winston-Salem, the city where Krispy Kreme is headquartered.

"One of the biggest ways they grab people is by sampling," says Mishra, an adjunct marketing professor who counts herself among Krispy Kreme's customer evangelists. "It's ingenious and simple." [23]

Indeed, Krispy Kreme has mastered the concept of the bite-size chunk. Haven't tried that new New York cheescake doughnut? Chances are the clerk behind the counter will fix that.

"Here, try one," he says.

Buying a dozen of the original glazed? Store employees often include an extra hot one wrapped in a napkin. It's a reward for waiting in line. Or for smiling. Or for being a repeat customer. In marketing terms, it's creating customer delight.

At new store openings, Krispy Kreme employees satiate the throngs of people in line with samples. The goodwill of a free doughnut carries enormous cachet.

But wait, there's more: To say hello to the neighborhood, the manager of a new store visits nearby homes and businesses, handing out doughnuts like a culinary pied piper. On the day Krispy Kreme's stock trading switched from the Nasdaq to the New York Stock Exchange, the company blocked off part of Wall Street and set up an outdoor doughnut-making theater. That day, the company gave away 40,000 doughnuts and 17,000 cups of coffee. It also had the second highest performing initial public offering of 2000.

"It was a phenomenal response," Parker says. "I think the reaction to that really helped us understand how the mobile store could help us extend the hot doughnuts "now" experience." [24]

Giving away tens of thousands of doughnuts each year creates two easily identifiable results.

1. Customer goodwill
2. Enormous buzz

"If you're going to use word of mouth as your marketing strategy, you have to have a good product," Mishra says. "That's the biggest component to success. Krispy Kreme has an outstanding product, and it's so consistently good." [25]

As Krispy Kreme continually confounds Wall Street and turns the traditional retail and fast-food marketing world upside down with its antiadvertising bias, Parker admits that the company's marketing success is not due to any master plan.

"Evolution is the way to describe the marketing strategy, not revolution," he says.[26]

Lessons learned:

- Master the bite-size chunk; let customers sample your product in creative and fun venues.
- A marketing strategy is evolutionary, not revolutionary.

EVANGELISM SCORECARD: KRISPY KREME DOUGHNUTS

Customer Plus-Delta

- The company receives 6,000 e-mails a month with stories about writers' first Krispy Kreme experience as well as suggestions for improvement and ideas for new store locations.
- The company Web site actively encourages feedback on all aspects of its operations.
- Each store is graded weekly on its product, presentation, and customer service.

Napsterized Knowledge

- The doughnut-making process is open for customers to see.

Build the Buzz

- Its outstanding product generates tremendous levels of word-of-mouth advertising.
- PR efforts surrounding each store opening typically create media countdowns to the event.
- Company executives make themselves widely available during store openings to capitalize on the media interest surrounding the openings.
- Its mobile doughnut machine, which debuted in 2002, takes the Krispy Kreme experience on the road to places where Krispy Kreme has not yet materialized.

Create Community

- The company promotes fundraising efforts all over the U.S. by selling discounted doughnuts to cause-related groups and allowing them to resell them at full retail price or higher.

Bite-Size Chunks

- Each store gives away thousands of doughnuts each year as part of its sampling strategy.
- Stores are generous in handing out extras for people waiting in line.

Create a Cause

- Its marketing focuses on the emotional connection customers feel, not on the product.

Coordinates

Company:	Krispy Kreme Doughnuts, Inc.
Headquarters:	Winston-Salem, N.C.
Founded:	1937
President:	Scott Livengood
Marketing chief:	Stan Parker
Description:	Hot Doughnuts Now
Industry:	Restaurant/Retail
Employees:	3,200
Ownership:	Publicly traded (NYSE:KKD)
Web site:	<www.krispykreme.com>

CHAPTER | # 10

THE HIGH-FLYING SOLUTIONMAN
solutionpeople

"Judge intelligence by the answers given to questions. Judge creativity by the questions asked." [1]

—GERALD HAMAN, founder and president of SolutionPeople

Gerald Haman spent $2,500 to launch his million-dollar business.

Haman's company is SolutionPeople, a Chicago-based creativity, innovation, training, and consulting firm. It helps companies brainstorm ideas for new products and services, solve existing problems, and improve teamwork skills. Haman launched SolutionPeople not long after the elder George Bush was being sworn in as president. Haman's idea behind his company: training should be fun, and the tools for it should be perpetually useful.

It was 1989 and Haman bet that investing a few thousand dollars to mingle with the 5,000 attendees at the meeting of the American Society for Training and Development (ASTD) at the Dallas, Texas, Convention Center would be a good strategy for launching his company. The human resources and training professionals who make up the ASTD get together every year to discuss the latest techniques and methodologies to train people in their companies.

Haman had a product that generated a lot of buzz: a handheld tool he called the Pocket Innovator that training professionals could carry in their pocket. Like a deck of cards but with a binding, the card in the Pocket

Innovator was filled with provocative questions that would spur its users to think about their problem creatively.

So, it's 1989 at the ASTD convention, and Haman's booth is next to that of Ned Herrmann, a well-known creativity specialist whose book *Creative Brain* had just been released. Herrmann was a biggie in the business during his career and, in Haman's eyes, a giant who could squash all upstarts. Was it an omen?

"I've never even thought of putting myself in the same class as Herrmann because he was such a pioneer in the field," Haman says. "A lot of his research is a model for ours. His thinking influenced mine. And we were at the same conference in Dallas. That's interesting; I've never thought of that before but yes, I think it was an omen."[2]

This moment in Haman's history did not come lightly. He bootstrapped his company from the outset. To save on expenses, he had recruited his sister, Elaine, to staff the convention booth with him, and they took turns going to the bathroom. But Haman's bet paid off as people lined up dozens deep to purchase the Pocket Innovator. Buzz about the little tool spread quickly on the trade show's floor.

"I think we captured some attention for having a unique tool that people wanted to get their hands on," Haman concedes. "If there's one theme that has allowed us to have people walk away as evangelists is everybody gets a tool that can help them to a certain degree."[3]

Because his product got people talking, two key things happened as a result of the conference: (1) Haman landed two big clients: Hewlett Packard and Digital Equipment Corporation; and (2) he met Linda Stockman-Vines, a writer, who played a central role in helping create huge amounts of buzz for the company.

As a company of one, Haman eventually signed up 50 clients from that weeklong show in Dallas. The tool and Haman's company were instant hits. Did his confidence ever waver before the show?

"I wasn't nervous," he says. "I was excited and intuitively felt it would be successful."[4]

He grossed $87,000 his first year in business. Twelve years later in 2002, SolutionPeople was doing $4 million per year and occupying several studios in a converted warehouse in Chicago's West Loop. At the beginning of 2002, he counted 160 of the Fortune 500 among his clients. He charges between $60,000 to $100,000 for two and three days of brainstorming facilitation. His annual growth rate between 1999 and 2001 was 30 percent; and Haman keeps a staff of ten people very, very busy.

When he launched the company, Haman had few competitors in what's loosely called the "creativity consulting" industry. In 2002, the landscape of consultants who take organizations through a systematic creativity process is filled with competitors big and small, from McKinsey to Eureka Ranch and Gary Hamel's Strategos.

Haman's work has taken him all over the world, including Singapore, where he helped 7,500 people at a stadium generate 454,000 ideas in 60 minutes. There he set three Guinness World Records: the highest volume of ideas generated in 60 minutes; the largest brainstorming team ever assembled; and the largest team of facilitators ever assembled. A survey conducted by Northwestern University's Kellogg Alumni Consulting Group reported that SolutionPeople has helped its clients generate over 1 million ideas valued at $1 billion dollars.

Haman keeps a framed copy of his first paycheck—a $29,000 endorsement from Digital Equipment—in his office. His marketing methodology from the beginning was to investigate what people needed and then to create tools and ideas to meet those needs.

SolutionPeople creates customer evangelists because:

- A unique and helpful tool gets people talking.
- Haman focuses on building networks of fans.
- Expert media relations help fuel interest and belief in his cause.
- Business is theater—SolutionPeople provides a memorable experience.

Let's examine in detail each of these ways by which SolutionPeople creates customer evangelists.

HOW A UNIQUE AND HELPFUL TOOL GETS PEOPLE TALKING

Gerald Haman has always been on the creative side of business. In the early 1980s, he was a concert promoter for Air Supply and Cheap Trick. Tiring of the road, he landed at Procter & Gamble in 1982, selling Crest and Scope.

He migrated to Big Five consulting firm Arthur Andersen in 1987, where he was a researcher in the company's Professional Education Division. It was at Andersen that Haman's ideas for his own company started to take shape.

Frustrated that few people at Andersen seemed to care much for the overweight training manuals the company issued in bulky three-ring binders, Haman decided to test a hypothesis: Did anyone really use the things?

"The firm was spending millions of dollars a year on training materials," he says. "The only people who seemed to appreciate them were the people who designed them. They would go in for their performance reviews and say,

'Yeah, I developed this one-day seminar, and here's my big, fat three-ring binder. Look what I accomplished.' "[5]

Being the Big Five consulting professional he was at the time, Haman launched a formal study. His hunch that the girth of the training binders made them impractical to use consistently proved right. One day, while shopping in a tile store, Haman picked up a swatch of tile color samples, and the proverbial lightbulb—Haman's trademark icon—clicked on. How about a training tool that could fit in one's pocket yet provide structure for the creative process? With that, the Pocket Innovator tool—which eventually became the KnowBrainer tool—was born. (See Figure 10.1.)

Like those color sample strips in Figure 10.1, the KnowBrainer tool performs in the same type of theater. Imagine 96 of the strips bolted together with information on each side. Add scads of descriptive phrases and provocative questions such as, "What is needed, wanted, or wished?" or "What should people KNOW?" Organize them according to four strategic

Figure 10.1 | **The KnowBrainer**

categories of "Investigate, Create, Evaluate, and Activate" (what Haman calls the Diamond Solution Process), and you have the KnowBrainer tool.

What makes the tool a strategic and viral element of Haman's marketing prowess? For starters, it's portable, slipping easily into a purse, a pocket, or a palm. It's unlike most other training tools, although the KnowBrainer seems familiar—just like holding those color swatches from the tile or paint store.

In evangelism marketing terms, the KnowBrainer tool is a Napsterized version of Haman's knowledge. Using it day to day doesn't require a $150 per hour consultant (although it can help).

"My attitude has been to get as many of these out there as possible so that people talk about them," Haman says. "Napsterized is a good way to think about it. If you think about the ease of sharing, that's key, although these are difficult to photocopy, and I don't know if people would go through the work of copying one of these, which has been one of the clever aspects about it."[6]

In addition, the KnowBrainer works pretty well as a sales tool for landing future customers. Haman ships the KnowBrainer to prospects in advance of their meeting and uses it to discover the companies' problems and issues. "It always makes for an engaging discussion," Haman says.[7]

With SolutionPeople clearly labeled on each KnowBrainer, the tool reminds its users—whether they have met Haman or not—of its origin. Unlike most traditional marketing trinkets, this one provides real value.

"What makes it viral is that it feels pretty good to have in the palm of your hand. It just feels comfortable to have around to play with. But if everyone can generate some ideas that are useful, they're going to tell other people and say, 'Hey, this helped me; it might help you.' Then I think the virality potential is really good."[8]

Twelve years after their creation, Haman estimates he has sold roughly 150,000 copies of the pocket-based tools.

Lessons learned:

- Understand and study what doesn't work in your industry.
- Your product or service must be unique and deliver immediate value.
- Size matters; in this case, smaller is better.

HAMAN'S FOCUS ON BUILDING NETWORKS OF FANS

Haman launched SolutionPeople without four-color brochures or a Web site (it was 1989, after all) and not much marketing collateral: just a well-defined service, a solid elevator pitch, and a contagious tool that created buzz. "We didn't even have a letterhead until about two years after we started," Haman says.[9]

For those who labor under an assumption that growth comes from advertising strategies dedicated to "creating brand awareness and building brand equity," Haman's success is evidence that a grassroots approach can build a long-term, sustainable company. It can even work for a company that wishes to remain small, which is Haman's objective.

"Can I imagine having built my business through advertising?" Haman asks, then laughs. "It's kind of fun to think about it, I imagine. But no, I can't."[10]

Thirteen years after SolutionPeople landed its first customer, the company still lacks four-color brochures. Other than its Web site, <www.solutionpeople.com>, the company has not produced any sales collateral. Haman has grown his business through three types of marketing connections (not in any particular order of importance).

1. Membership in organizations
2. Appearances at conferences and networking events
3. Referrals from friends and associates

To understand his success with grassroots marketing, let's begin with the personal, people-based evangelism that SolutionPeople has enjoyed. We spend a few hours with Haman in the "Thinkubator," Haman's name for his studio, to trace the routes that have led to his client engagements.

Because Haman maintains a database of nearly everyone he's met, we're able to build diagrams of the connections. We create a detailed network map of people, association memberships, and speaking engagements. Three hours later, we have scribbled names, dates, companies, and events on five large easel sheets. We leave the Thinkubator convinced that even one person can create a confluence of connections and a roster of paying clients.

Take, for instance, Dan Pink, the author of *Free Agent Nation,* a book about the growing ranks of the self-employed in the United States. At one point in his career, Pink was the chief speechwriter for Vice President Al Gore.

He's also a contributing editor for *Fast Company* magazine as well as what author Emanuel Rosen calls a "network hub": a person of influence whom people rely on for information. Haman calls Pink "a master networker."

In 1998, Pink posted a note to *Fast Company*'s online communities, which are known as Company of Friends cells (see Chapter 6). At the time, Pink was conducting research for *Free Agent Nation* and visiting Company of Friends cells around the country to meet free agents.

Enter Neil Kane, a friend of Haman's since the early 1990s. Kane told Haman about the online note and encouraged Haman to contact Pink. Haman did, and they enjoyed a good conversation. As a result, Pink recommended to his colleagues at *Fast Company* that SolutionPeople would make an interesting magazine story.

The *Fast Company* editors were intrigued. A few months later, in April 1999, the magazine featured a three-page article about life in the Thinkubator. The 769-word article in *Fast Company*, which included a color photograph of Haman dressed as his superhero alter ego "Solutionman," was directly responsible for landing nine clients, eight of them Fortune 500 companies.

Let's trace the web of connections from that single, evangelistic response Neil Kane posted in reply to Dan Pink's question as shown in Figure 10.2 and the 12 steps depicted in the figure.

1. Dan Pink posts a question to a Company of Friends list.
2. Neil Kane notices the post and forwards it to Haman.
3. An article about Haman is written for the magazine.
4. An employee of Adidas reads the *Fast Company* article and calls Haman for more information. Adidas becomes a client.
5. An employee of Adidas loves the work and evangelizes SolutionPeople to contacts at Harvard University, several of whose MBA graduates eventually become SolutionPeople clients.
6. A representative of a company called Momentum Marketing reads the article and decides SolutionPeople is just what its client, General Motors, needs. Several weeks later, the Buick division of GM joins the SolutionPeople client roster.
7. Fast Company invites Haman to speak at its 1999 RealTime conference in Naples, Florida.
8. At the conference, Fast Company gives away 500 KnowBrainer tools to attendees. The tool giveaway is central to landing new clients General Electric, American Express, and the Tom Peters Group.
9. At the RealTime convention, Haman meets Andy Hines, who at the time was with Kellogg's. Several weeks later, a team from Kellogg's journeys from their Battle Creek, Michigan, headquarters for a session at the Thinkubator. Their brainstorm eventually produces new cereal products.
10. Hines departs Kellogg's and joins Dow Chemical. Shortly thereafter, Dow becomes a SolutionPeople client.
11. Hines evangelizes Haman's company to his peers in the chemical industry, and eight months later Haman is speaking before the Chemical Specialties Conference in Chicago.

Figure 10.2 | **Web of Connections from One Evangelist**

Source: SolutionPeople

12. Sitting in the front row at the conference was an executive from Capital One, the financial services firm. The executive liked what he heard and shortly thereafter a Capital One team was jamming in the Thinkubator, brainstorming new products and ideas.

All told, one evangelist—Neil Kane—was indirectly responsible for at least $2 million in revenue for SolutionPeople.

How Two Davids Partnered to Help Goliath

Kevin Olsen is the founding partner of One Smooth Stone, a strategic communications and marketing firm that works primarily in the meetings and events industry. In 1995, Olsen took the same calculated risk Haman had three years earlier by investing several thousand dollars in a trade show as a bet-the-company marketing strategy. But the trade show, the Chicago Society of Association Executives, was a bust. "We couldn't catch a cold there," he says. "And we only met one person. It was Gerald."

"We were ready for Gerald."

It turns out that Olsen and his young company needed the systematic approach toward creativity and innovation that Haman offered. The two became fast friends. Olsen involved Haman in several of his company's projects, and as they worked together, they referred clients to one another. There was Xerox, A.T. Kearney, Navistar, Motorola.

Olsen quickly grasped the idea of evangelism marketing—it turned out that he is the son of a preacher.

"An evangelist is one of the highest callings there is," he says. "I am an evangelist of what I believe in: building relationships that win. Gerald is a classic example of a relationship that will have legs for a long time."[12]

Lessons learned:

- Cultivate relationships of quality, not quantity.
- Keep good records of people you meet.
- Help your friends as much as possible.
- Get involved with organizations you believe in.

EXPERT MEDIA RELATIONS HELP FUEL INTEREST AND BELIEF IN HAMAN'S CAUSE

The power of the media can be exponential, and Haman has created a solid strategy to help journalists quickly accomplish what many of them seek: a good story about a colorful character.

He sends the KnowBrainer tool to reporters before an interview and uses it during the interview as a live demonstration of the tool's effectiveness as well as for providing reporters a new avenue for asking questions.

The first article about SolutionPeople in 1989 created ripples of subsequent articles that continues years later. Haman met Linda Stockman-Vines, a journalist who writes about training, human resources, and creativity issues, in 1989 at the ASTD conference in Dallas. Intrigued,

Stockman-Vines wrote an article about the KnowBrainer tool for *Human Resource Executive* magazine. We can trace the effects Stockman-Vines had on Haman's business and the roots of SolutionPeople at the 1989 ASTD convention by examining Figure 10.3 and a chronology of the 12 steps represented in the figure.

1. Haman rents a booth at the ASTD conference in Dallas.
2. Five hundred people purchase the KnowBrainer tool (known then as the Pocket Innovator).
3. Hewlett Packard and Digital Equipment Corporation become clients.

Figure 10.3 | **Early Roots of SolutionPeople**

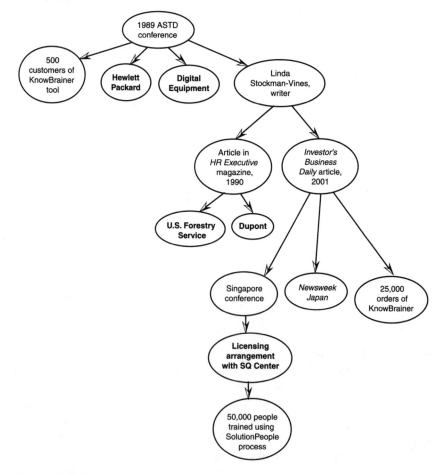

Source: SolutionPeople

4. Haman meets writer Linda Stockman-Vines.
5. She writes an article about Haman for *Human Resource Executive* magazine.
6. Executives at Dupont and the U.S. Forest Service read the article and sign on as SolutionPeople clients.
7. In 2001, Stockman-Vines writes another article about Haman, this time for *Investor's Business Daily*.
8. An official with the government of Singapore reads the second article and invites Haman to help brainstorm government improvement strategies, which leads in turn to setting a Guinness World Record.
9. The Singapore conference leads to a KnowBrainer licensing arrangement (and one of Haman's key strategic objectives) with a Singaporean company.
10. The Singapore licensing arrangement trains 50,000 people in Asia using the SolutionPeople approach.
11. *Newsweek Japan* publishes an article on Haman's company, an Indonesian consulting firm that reads the article licenses the KnowBrainer tool.
12. Haman sells thousands of KnowBrainer tools because of the *Investor's Business Daily* article.

Lessons learned:

• Talk to the media at every opportunity.
• Help the media tell a good story—don't expect them to blindly promote you.

BUSINESS AS THEATER: PROVIDE A MEMORABLE EXPERIENCE

Gerald Haman is not afraid to be out there. To dress up in a costume; to stand out in the crowded business field; to introduce theater into business.

Meet Solutionman.

Solutionman sports a red cape, tights, and a sturdy chin not unlike Haman's boyhood hero, Superman. Solutionman was born when Lari Washburn, one of Haman's clients at Lucent, said out of the blue one day, "You're such a solution man." That was another lightbulb moment, and soon Solutionman was being photographed for *Fast Company* magazine, making appearances in schools, and canvassing trade shows.

An appearance at Chicago's Francis Xavier Ward grade school in 1997 created a good deal of buzz. Solutionman teaches kids in various

Chicago schools several times a year about the value of teamwork and creativity. He also has pictures made with the kids he teaches, and the pictures are developed with a Solutionman sticker on the back. One photograph caught the attention of a parent who wondered what the Solutionman business was about and called Haman for more information. The parent, a lawyer for a large Chicago-based law firm, liked the pitch and thought the American Bar Association (ABA) could use Solutionman's help. Soon, the ABA was a client and later the parent's law firm itself.

The creation of Solutionman is part of a larger network of connections in the history of Haman's company that began years earlier with Haman's membership in Chicago's Museum of Contemporary Art, as depicted in Figure 10.4 and explained in the following 11 steps.

1. Haman joins Chicago's Museum of Contemporary Art.
2. He becomes active in the museum's group of art evangelists.
3. His involvement with the group introduces him to several future clients: R.R. Donnelly, the large printing company, and two advertising agencies: J. Walter Thompson and DDB.
4. His involvement with the museum inspires him to pursue his hobby of painting.
5. His hobby results in two exhibitions.
6. At one of the exhibitions, Haman meets two future clients, Helene Curtis and Discover Card. He is also invited to participate in another art exhibition called Around the Coyote.
7. At another exhibition, he meets his future wife, Jillian.
8. At Around the Coyote, Haman meets Val Mrak, a film producer, who introduces him to Mary Borse, at that time an employee of AT&T, which later becomes a client.
9. AT&T invites him to speak at a conference, where he meets Lari Washburn of Lucent, which soon becomes a client. His work with Lari leads to the development of Solutionman.
10. At an appearance at a Chicago school, Solutionman's picture piques the interest of a parent, who eventually helps Haman land new business with the American Bar Association and a large Chicago-based law firm.
11. Solutionman inspires the creation of a huge lightbulb display, which gets the attention of a Chicago networking group (First Tuesday), and eventually leads to landing another client, Guinness UDV, the beverage company.

Figure 10.4 | **SolutionPeople Buzz Map**

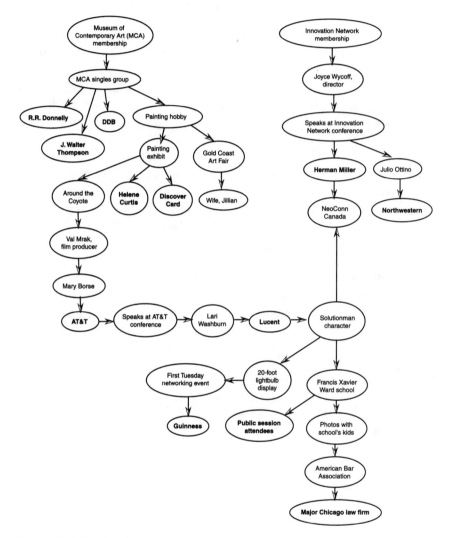

Source: SolutionPeople

After each major event, SolutionPeople posts a 100-page, picture-heavy PowerPoint document on its Web site. The photos prominently feature people and the event's accomplishments. A 20-person event held at an English castle in March 2002 generated 5,000 viewings of the online document, Haman says.

Life in the Thinkubator Theater

A common element among our seven case study companies is an unwavering emphasis on an enjoyable experience. A utilitarian experience is not memorable, but an enjoyable and fun experience creates buzz. A day at the Thinkubator, Haman's name for his studio where people journey to brainstorm ideas for their companies, gets people talking. Coauthor Jackie Huba signed up for an Accelerated Innovation seminar held in October 2001.

A week before I am to attend the seminar at the Chicago-based Thinkubator, I receive a "KnowBrainer Pre-Seminar Planner" via e-mail. It asks nine questions about my understanding of creativity and innovation and how I might apply what I learn. I'm asked to send back the answers before the seminar.

Training day: Once inside the Thinkubator's front door, I'm mesmerized. A toy frog at the entrance delivers a welcome croak. The room is a colorful splash of life. Everything from the furniture—large, red-lip chairs and comfy couches—to the dozens of lightbulbs-as-idea sculptures to a bathroom whose tub doubles as a tank for Solutionfish creates brainstorm sparks. It's like stepping in to Pee Wee Herman's Playhouse minus the talking chair. I can't wait to talk about everything in the room being crazily out of the ordinary.

It's 8 AM, and the other workshop attendees are already jazzed; music jukes the background. We settle in on the comfy funky couches and beanbag chairs. Haman introduces himself to our group of 25. We are marketing specialists, organizational development consultants, executives of associations, and managers of various companies in and outside of Chicago. We learn this will be a bite-size chunk of what Haman's Fortune 500 clients pay up to $100,000 to experience over several days.

Haman explains that one day during his junior year at the University of North Dakota he arrived late at his philosophy class. His professor, Dr. Benjamin Ring, was not pleased and asked Haman to consider the question What motivates people? By the end of class, Haman had written that question over and over until he filled 25 pages of his notebook. (Interestingly, Dr. Ring had also posed the same question to a previous student, former NBA star and renowned coach Phil Jackson.) In 1981, the question of what motivates people burned inside Haman's mind, eventually driving him to launch SolutionPeople. The answer to the question: being creative.

Thanks to a study by a graduate student at Northwestern University, Haman learned that people are 13 percent more productive when not wearing shoes, and 20 percent of people think faster when standing. Haman invites us to remove our shoes and slip on brand-new white tube socks that he gleefully distributes. Everyone is quite amused.

It's time for work. We begin with the "Know Your Brain" game. We file into a room filled with color-coded cards—blue, red, green, yellow—each of which has a word imprinted on it. We are told to pick three cards that best describe ourselves. I select two reds (Enthusiastic, Passionate) and a green (Planner). We file back into the main room and introduce ourselves, our colors, and why we chose the colors we did. As I circulate in the room, I make connections with my fellow reds, knowing that we belong to a community of passion.

Haman keeps the motivation mojo going by announcing he will distribute tickets to those who actively participate in today's session by asking questions or volunteering. (It seems Dr. Ring has taught him well.) At the end of the day, he will conduct a drawing for prizes for people who gather the most tickets. Immediately, we're intrigued. Win prizes? This is going to be fun.

Haman tells how Einstein was once asked: If you were given an hour to save the world, how would you spend the time? Einstein said he would spend 55 minutes investigating the problems and 5 minutes coming up with ideas.

He says, "Judge intelligence by the answers given to questions. Judge creativity by the questions asked."[13]

This is a segue into the "Question" game. We are each to pair up with someone and practice using the "Flash Word" technique, just as Haman does with real reporters. I pair up with John, whose firm helps companies improve shareholder value. One of us is to play the "reporter" and the other an "expert." Using the tool, John plays reporter first and randomly asks questions from each of the four steps in the process. I'm stumped by several questions. The KnowBrainer surfaces issues I would have never imagined, especially in my profession.

The challenge is dialed up a notch because John takes satisfaction from playing mean reporter. I find the KnowBrainer such questions as "What do you want people to feel?" and "What do you want people to think?" interesting because they're uncommon. John throws in his own, with some derisiveness: "Why would anyone care about what you do?" I guess that my answers don't immediately add up to shareholder value. I decide that John could have a new career on Fox News.

Now it's time to form "colorful teams of twisted thinkers." We organize into groups of four and five. Our mission is to apply Haman's Diamond Solution Process to a problem. We tackle "how to choose a Halloween costume." Our group does OK in the investigative and creative steps, but falters in the evaluative step, and we're not sure why, even though our problem seems straightforward.

The metaphor of how this happens every day in companies across the world—settle on an idea and move forward—is not lost on us.

By now it's time for lunch, which is being served in the Thinkubator's disco, which is part dance floor and part carnival. Freed from our natural adult states, we play with some of the toys, such as the basketball shoot. Music, of course, is playing. We gather around three large round tables with white tablecloths and heavy silverware. Food is gourmet and so is the conversation. When I ask the eight people at my table how they heard about Haman and SolutionPeople they reply it was from another person.

Most are here to experience the Solutionman's creativity and brainstorming exercises firsthand as a toe-in-the-water reconnaissance mission to evaluate SolutionPeople for a full, three-day session, or to hire Haman as a speaker for their conference. All have paid to be here. The idea of the bite-size chunk works beautifully for the Thinkubator.

After lunch, it's time for karaoke. We divide into teams and take turns singing lead and backup for several songs that everyone knows. There's nothing quite like belting out "Takin' Care of Business" at the top of your lungs after lunch to stave off the effects of turkey sandwich tryptophan. We venture back to the Thinkubator to work through the Diamond Solution Process on our individual projects.

Once finished, Haman poses a to-the-point question: How many of us brainstormed an idea that will make $5,000? $10,000? $50,000? One participant says his idea could generate $1 million. This has everyone's attention. By positioning our work in terms of returned revenue, Haman deftly illustrates the relationship between creativity and making it pay. Marketing is the same; it should have well-defined returns for each idea invested.

Are we ready for the "Thinkathon," Haman asks. He distributes sheets filled with lightbulbs that represent ideas for a problem that's posed at the top of the sheet. Each lightbulb represents an idea of how to tackle the problem. Haman tells us about his customer at Abbot Labs, the large pharmaceutical company: The customer tapes Haman's lightbulb sheet to the door of his office, with a problem/challenge at the top. All visitors must add an idea to the sheet before entering his office.

Haman distributes sheets filled with drawings of lightbulbs. Our challenge is to think of ways to introduce more creativity into our workplace. We have three minutes to brainstorm ideas. When our time is up, we pass our sheet to the person on our left and add ideas to the problem that has just been handed to us from the person on our right.

It's the end of the day and time for the prize drawing. Good thing, too; by now we're brain dead. Prizes are think bars, lightbulb toys, squeezable brains, and Einstein paraphernalia. Haman gives everyone a hat that looks like a brain, with everyone designated a "brainiac."

An expert marketer, Haman reminds us about the value we received during this day of creativity.

- A binder with models of how creativity and innovation work
- Our own KnowBrainer tool
- Thinkathon template sheets (lightbulb sheets)
- A small notepad to capture ideas (with an extra paper replacement pack)
- Ideas from our individual projects that should return actual value

He also tells us we'll receive an e-mail survey asking us to rate the session. Even though we're exhausted, many of us find it hard to leave. We're in a cool and creative space, where we had fun, led by a warm and smart leader, and we met some great people. Some linger to inquire about Haman's ability to help them with their companies.

For many of the assembled participants, leaving meant going back to a job and office politics and a decided lack of creativity. Armed with the tools and knowledge of the session, they hope to change that. All of them will tell others about the workout their brains received.

Lessons learned:

- Gathering pre- and postexperience feedback is valuable.
- Give customers opportunities to meet one another.
- Comfort is more valuable than style.
- Fun matters.
- Provide sampling opportunities during every step of your sales process.

EVANGELISM SCORECARD: SOLUTIONPEOPLE

Customer Plus-Delta

- Every customer is given the opportunity to grade her experience.
- Quantitative and qualitative data are gathered, collated, and reviewed.

Napsterized Knowledge

- The KnowBrainer tool is a handheld encapsulation of Haman's methodology.
- By creating an interactive experience, Haman has provided the means and the tools for customers to conduct better brainstorms in their own companies.

Build the Buzz

- A unique product spreads buzz quickly.
- A positive and fun experience spreads buzz quickly, especially with the media.

Create Community

- Participating at the Thinkubator is joining a community for a day.
- Displaying talents within a community creates connections.

Bite-Size Chunks

- For those who are uncertain about investing $100,000 for a dedicated session, a company representative can first attend a daylong public session for several hundred dollars.

Create a Cause

- Haman launched his company to help people discover their creative potential.

Coordinates

Company:	SolutionPeople
Headquarters:	Chicago, Illinois
President:	Gerald Haman
Marketing chief:	Scott Buchanan (who started after the completion of this book)
Description:	A creativity, innovation, training, and consulting firm
Industry:	Training and development
Employees:	10
Ownership:	Privately held
Web site:	<www.solutionpeople.com>

CHAPTER 11

THE HISTORY LESSONS OF O'REILLY'S WARS
o'reilly & associates

*"People are going to change the world and accelerate change
by spreading their knowledge."*[1]

—TIM O'REILLY, founder and president of publishing company O'Reilly & Associates

Sebastopol, California, was named after a fistfight.

Legend has it that in 1855 an argument between two early settlers in northern California, Jeff Stevens and a man known only as Hibbs, erupted into fisticuffs. It was a lengthy match, with Hibbs taking the majority of punches thrown. Beaten and bloodied, Hibbs staggered in retreat to the general store, barricading himself inside for the rest of the day. Thwarted after several hours of waiting him out, Stevens finally went home a victor but defeated by Hibbs's retreat.[2]

The spectacle of the fight reminded amused onlookers of the Crimean War, which had been raging half a world away. Back then, the French and the Russians disagreed over who should have access to trade routes in the Middle East. Czar Nicholas of Russia wanted to protect his religious shrines along the routes at all costs. As disputes involving religion often do, the disagreement erupted into war. Britain and France teamed up to take on the Russians. Britain's Florence Nightingale tagged along as a medical technician, eventually changing the nature of nursing.[3]

The French and the British chased the Russians all the way back to the Russian naval base of Sevastopol and could have considered their mission accomplished and gone home. But they didn't. At Sevastopol (where the *v* is favored over the *b*) the Russians picked off the British and French like ducks at a hypnotic pond. Their barricade was impenetrable, and Nightingale had her hands full. Two years later, the British and French gave up and went home defeated. The primary lesson of the Crimean War: don't be greedy.

How ironic then that 144 years later a few residents of quiet Sebastopol, California, had their own Crimean War. This time the battle was with an Internet giant to the north, Seattle-based Amazon.com and its founder, "Czar" Jeff Bezos.

Amazon was granted a patent for its "One-Click" buying process, which can significantly reduce the time required for online purchases. Amazon wanted to enforce its patent and make its biggest competitor, Barnes & Noble, stop using a similar process. Fear that Amazon would enforce its patent against other Web sites also using a one-click program filtered across the Internet. It was like Czar Nicholas seeking to protect his trade routes at all costs.

Enter Tim O'Reilly.

He is the founder and CEO of O'Reilly & Associates, a publishing company based in Sebastopol, California. From its beginnings as a technical writing consultancy, O'Reilly & Associates—often referred to as ORA by people inside and outside the company—has blossomed into arguably the most respected technical publisher today. Its growth has fueled an expansion into medical, travel, and bioinformatics titles; conferences; and a brief foray into software. With 300 employees, O'Reilly & Associates is the biggest company in Birkenstock-bucolic Sebastopol—a $65 million company in 2000.

Tim O'Reilly describes his calling as an idealist who rallies technology mavens around causes that improve technology and its community of enthusiasts. When Amazon.com was granted its One-Click patent, O'Reilly began receiving calls asking to organize a boycott of Amazon. Instead, O'Reilly sent Bezos an e-mail that read, in part:

> The technologies that you have used to launch your amazing success would never have become widespread if the early web players, from Tim Berners-Lee on, had acted as you have acted in filing and enforcing this patent. Because, of course, you are not the only one who can play the patent game. And once the web becomes fenced in by competing patents and other attempts to make this glorious open playing field into a proprietary wasteland, the springs of further innovation will dry up. In short, I think you're pissing in the well.[4]

O'Reilly says that Bezos replied with a terse "corporate brush-off" e-mail that held Amazon's ground. Undaunted, O'Reilly created a petition to protest Amazon's patent, which he e-mailed to several influential technology leaders with strong followings, encouraging them to sign and forward the petition.

"I knew that if I sent this e-mail message to a few people, they would reflect on it, and I would get . . . critical mass all at once, where all these people are hearing the same message at the same time," O'Reilly says. "It's a refinement of the principle that if you can get that critical mass of recognition coming from multiple directions at once, you're in good shape."[5]

Two days later, O'Reilly's evangelism for the cause had resulted in collecting more than 10,000 signatures. Thousands of comments were paired with signatures, such as: "Dear Mr. Bezos: I think that your efforts to maintain and enforce the One-Click patent are a mistake, which makes me question whether I want to continue working with Amazon.com."[6]

Bezos paid attention. After a phone call with Bezos that O'Reilly describes as cordial and informative, Bezos agreed to drop his enforcement of Amazon's One-Click patent. Like Florence Nightingale 150 years earlier, Tim O'Reilly had saved Amazon from itself while evangelizing a convenient feature of Internet commerce that many take for granted today.

It's this caused-based leadership in a public arena filled with posturing and wrestlerlike catcalls (where most of the participants lack muscle tone and all of them wear glasses) that has made O'Reilly & Associates a leader in its field. It has also been a large component of the company's marketing strategy.

O'Reilly & Associates creates customer evangelists because:

- Its marketing strategy is largely built on advocacy.
- Customer communities are central to its success.
- Vast amounts of its knowledge are available outside its core products.
- Customer feedback drives product improvement and innovation.

BUILDING A MARKETING STRATEGY LARGELY ON ADVOCACY

Tim O'Reilly's advocacy of technology causes began in July 1996 when Microsoft had just pissed him off.

Back then, Microsoft had two versions of its high-level operating system available: NT Workstation and NT Server. Whereas NT Server was more feature-rich of the two, both could function as Web servers. At the last minute, Microsoft changed the TCP-IP code on NT Workstation so that no more than ten computers could connect to it, essentially rendering it useless as a Web server. The upshot was that Microsoft doesn't own TCP-IP code; no one does. It's maintained by a volunteer group of programmers who help set and write to industrywide computer standards.

Microsoft's tactic effectively blocked Web-based software, including O'Reilly's, from being hosted on Microsoft's less expensive, yet popular, platform. Its ploy was to force owners to upgrade to the more expensive NT Server, which had no limitation on connections.

To Tim O'Reilly, Microsoft's action was a gambit to take control of the Internet.

"I was outraged," O'Reilly says. He channeled his outrage into a protest campaign that prominently featured him in several dozen news stories, including an appearance on CNN that he feared "went over most people's heads."

"I sent an open letter to all of our customers. I asked people to let Microsoft know this was cheesy. Microsoft got an awful lot of mail. I got an awful lot of mail from inside Microsoft saying 'Thank you for helping to do this. There's been a lot of internal debate here.'"[7]

A week later, Microsoft conceded to the protest campaign and removed the technical limitation. In the end, O'Reilly said, the only difference between the two products was "about three lines of code in the registry."

A month later, in August 1996, the U.S. Department of Justice received a formal complaint from an ad hoc consortium of technology companies about Microsoft's actions; history shows that O'Reilly's protest over NT Server was the opening act in an odyssey that culminated in 2001 when a federal judge declared that Microsoft was, indeed, a monopolist.

From the experience, O'Reilly realized that courting customers to be active participants in a cause that is of mutual benefit to company and customer is a central tenet of his business philosophy.

O'Reilly says: "This was accurate some years later in the whole Amazon patent protest—the idea of mobilizing a customer base. There is a level where you can have customer activists, people who care about the topic. A lot of what makes it work is that we draw our authors from the same customer pool. A classic statement about a market is . . . that it is a group of customers who reference each other when making buying decisions."[8]

Indeed, his company's marketing philosophy was crystallizing around this idea. At a publishing conference where he was asked to describe next-generation products such as eBooks, O'Reilly shared his epiphanous moment: "I said what's beyond the book is 'life and having an impact.' We got more and more excited about this idea that our fundamental mission wasn't to publish books. It was to capture knowledge and evangelize technologies. It was to capture the knowledge of innovators. People are going to change the world and accelerate change by spreading their knowledge."[9]

Sara Winge, O'Reilly's vice president of corporate communications, says of her boss: "Tim is real. He's coming from a belief of what's right."[10]

O'Reilly explains his interest in rallying his company around a cause another way: When he first met with distributors to sell his company's books overseas, he attended a prospective partner's executive conference; most of the talk was about money.

"I was just appalled," he says. "I said the reason you guys are always number two is because the only common language you have is money. All that your people talked about in this conference was how much money they were making or not making. There was no vision. If you follow the vision, you'll catch up on the money side."[11]

O'Reilly's advocacy on behalf of the open source community earned him *Infoworld*'s Industry Achievement Award in 1998. Asked to explain the roots of his activism, O'Reilly talks about his life. He was born in Cork, Ireland, in 1954. His father was an Irish neurologist, but the only way he could obtain a research professorship was if someone died and opened a slot. So the family moved to the United States when O'Reilly was six weeks old. As a teen, O'Reilly was a painfully shy "total nerd" and "the only kid who could strike out at kickball." Puberty and drama helped change that.

"I remember the first time I was on stage: my eyes would close down like the end of a Warner Brothers cartoon," he says. "I was close to fainting. I eventually trained myself to be an extrovert."[12] After high school, it was on to Harvard to study the classics. His honors thesis explored the tension between mysticism and logic in Plato's dialogues. O'Reilly notes that his wife, Christina, has been "a major influence"; her values are the company's values. This whole idea that the company is a meeting point of some work that's to be done to meet the needs of a group of people really came from her," he says.[13] With a wave of self-discovery having curled up to the shore, O'Reilly pauses. "Business is ultimately providing value. I look for the sweet spots where idealism meets making money."[14]

Because O'Reilly trained himself to be an extrovert, to be out there and take the stage for what he believes to be right, the lens of customer evangelism automatically is stronger and more focused.

Lessons learned:

- Work for the benefit of the customer community you serve.
- Campaigning on behalf of industry standards positions you as an industry leader.
- When in doubt, do the right thing.

CUSTOMER COMMUNITIES AS CENTRAL TO SUCCESS

The 7,700 residents of Sebastopol live in the heart of California's rich and sprawling wine country, 90 minutes north of the gleaming glass and satin metal office parks along Highway 101 that make up what is popularly known as Silicon Valley.

The 168,000 square feet spread among the three buildings that make up the headquarters of O'Reilly & Associates could easily be at home among ski chalets in Aspen. Built in 2001, company headquarters are very new; the rich aroma of new millwork fills the hallways. There's nothing office-park-like about the design and the layout, although there's plenty of room for the company to grow into.

The visitor lobby showcases the O'Reilly library of titles, a programmer's dream hutch. It's filled with the colorful spines of O'Reilly's technology books and the iconography of the animal etchings that identify most of the techie titles. Those bread-and-butter manuals cover a diverse range of subjects: *Programming Perl* to *SQL In a Nutshell* to *P2P Networking Overview* to the best-selling *Missing Manual* series.

The company's strategy is to court the communities of technologists whose livelihood depends on the technology concepts and code reviews in its books and manuals.

One courtship tactic is to publish 35 various and specialized weekly e-mail newsletters that cover topics like Linux, Java, and Perl; and there are special newsletters for librarians, professors, and book retailers as well. Each newsletter has its own voice imparted by an editor who is free to stamp his or her personality on its content. The newsletters also avoid a pushy sales approach. Tips are popular topics in O'Reilly newsletters, too, such as "Tips for Building Web Database Applications."

The company also actively courts the extensive online communities of technologists, such as the 2.5 million people who each month visit slashdot .org, a news and community site that posts links to articles of interest to programmers and engages in Web-based discussions about technology issues.

Jeff "Hemos" Bates, slashdot.org's executive editor, says that Tim O'Reilly's advocacy of technology causes is recognized by slashdot.org's community. "I think Tim's taking a stance on issues has definitely helped them," Bates says. "It has established [O'Reilly & Associates] as a company in which the management still 'gets it' and cares about the concerns of its readership. But frankly, it's the accessibility and intelligence of the people writing their books that really helps them. Those people, while having other jobs, burnish ORA's name because they are smart and connected with the community."[15]

O'Reilly & Associates learned how to connect with communities at a deeper level because of Brian Erwin, who had spent several years at Harper Collins in San Francisco and William Morrow in New York, marketing books like Alvin Toffler's *The Third Wave* and Christina Crawford's *Mommie Dearest*. Then came a call from the Sierra Club, a 700,000-member activist organization whose mission is to "Explore, enjoy and protect the planet," and Erwin launched its national media operation. It was a cause that suited Erwin well. His idealistic parents were "always taking in foster children or Peruvian refugees—it was just the nature of how I was raised," he says. "Each of us has an obligation to help those who aren't as lucky as we are."[16]

While at the Sierra Club, Erwin trained individuals and groups to fight companies and change government policies that needlessly harm the planet's ecosystem. Being surrounded by "the largest collection of Type A, outer-motivated, intelligent people I've ever been around" was an "incredible experience," Erwin says.[17]

Erwin joined O'Reilly as its director of public relations in 1992, just before the company published *The Whole Internet: User's Guide and Catalog*. It was a fortuitous engagement. Erwin used the tactics he had learned at the Sierra Club to market O'Reilly's products beyond its obvious channels.

"Before [Brian], we would have just sent the book out to regular trade magazines," Tim O'Reilly says.[18]

O'Reilly says that Erwin recognized the importance *The Whole Internet* could have for readers in understanding the role, capabilities, and potential of a global Internet with future implications for communications, commerce, and community. Erwin pursued coverage in such national media as *Time* magazine and the *New York Times* and sent copies to every member of Congress. According to O'Reilly:

> Brian really crystallized it for us because we were always part of a technical community. If you've ever done body surfing, you can see the waves coming. The point is, the essence of surfing is catching a wave at just the right moment and letting it carry you. A lot of customercentric marketing is catching waves. It first means watching the waves and being in touch with your market.
>
> One problem is that marketing is seen as an add-on as opposed to something that's intrinsic to the way you develop your products. While Brian got us to think about activism, we were on very fertile ground because we were already seeing ourselves as a voice of a community. We were writing the books for a class of people we knew really well because we were them.[19]

The Whole Internet was one of the first two books about a technological phenomenon that eventually spawned thousands of books, hundreds of magazines, and millions of Web sites. But the manuscript kept getting delayed, Erwin says, so in the summer of 1992 he decided to print 1,000 copies in its manuscript form to launch a grassroots campaign. He sent 500 copies to various media outlets and 500 to the moderators of news groups mentioned in the book with a personalized note attached that "would say 'We hope you enjoy this and we hope you'll speak well of it to others who are visiting your news group or mailing list.' Pretty soon we could see on the Internet that people were saying, 'Hey, we were mentioned here.' It spread exponentially."[20]

Erwin's strategy of identifying and targeting key influencers worked.

"That really is where the first wave of demand came from—from those who were already using the Internet,"[21] he says. The second wave came from the efforts of Sales Director Jill Tomich, whose grassroots activism with the company's network of retail booksellers turned corner bookstores into hubs for disseminating Internet information. She mounted campaigns that resulted in bookstores dedicating and naming shelf space for their growing list of Internet books, thus driving what became a multi-million-dollar publishing program.

Combining Erwin's evangelistic efforts with global media and financial markets with Tomich's local grassroots campaigns converged into a perfect storm of product demand. The book was selling 25,000 copies per month, Erwin says, and eventually sold more than a million copies. The New York Public Library named it "one of the most important books of the 20th century." The book eventually changed the nature of O'Reilly & Associates altogether. "It lifted the whole company financially and provided a focus for its next area of emphasis, which was away from operating systems and more towards mass communication," says Erwin.[22]

For Tim O'Reilly it was a marketing approach that codified the development of future programs. The search for key influencers started the process that "we have formalized as an evangelist program," O'Reilly says.[23] The O'Reilly evangelist program was launched in September 2000, with Simone Paddock named its first director.

"We saw that there was a possibility of seizing part of the marketing power in the community; we needed someone to create the community around O'Reilly,"[24] she says. The program, which is by invitation only, rewards the company's most visible evangelists with books, T-shirts, and discounts on O'Reilly conferences.

An O'Reilly evangelist is thus ordained because he stood up in an online discussion area, or a chat room, or in an Amazon book review and said he loves an O'Reilly title.

Although the company cannot specifically measure the effects of its evangelist program, it does have supporting evidence. Since the launch of the program, traffic to the company's Web site has doubled to 1.1 million visitors a month. During the first year of the evangelist program, O'Reilly's Web sites have been featured more than 70 times on slashdot.org; 20 of those notices were a direct result of an ordained O'Reilly evangelist. Considering that a single mention on slashdot.org can drive 10,000 to 20,000 unique visitors to oreilly.com, the evangelist program is spreading the word.

In 2002, the company launched the "O'Reilly Irregulars" program. For most publishers, understanding how much inventory exists in bookstores is a considerable, if not impossible, challenge. The "Irregulars" program relies on customers to report each month on how many books are sitting on the shelves of bookstores in medium and large cities. Within 72 hours of the program's announcement, the company had almost 300 volunteers, according to Sara Winge, the company's chief of corporate communications.

"We think one of the things that makes us stand out from our competitors is that we're better at listening to and talking with our customers," O'Reilly says. "We know that the people who read our books and Web sites and attend our conferences are also the people who are pushing the envelope of technology itself. They are the ones who lead, shape, and contribute to technical communities. Our mission is to pour fuel on the fire they're building."[25]

Lessons learned:

- Create communities within communities that cater to specialized knowledge.
- When it comes to your product, think like an activist: How can it change the world?
- Locate and embrace the best network hubs; ordain them as official evangelists.

VAST AMOUNTS OF ITS KNOWLEDGE ARE AVAILABLE OUTSIDE ITS CORE PRODUCTS

O'Reilly Napsterizes significant amounts of its company's knowledge outside a standard $39 technical book. The company maintains a network of 17 free Web sites filled with tools, knowledge, and information for programmers and information technology executives on a variety of techie topics.

For example, there's perl.com for people interested in the Perl programming language, which is used extensively for e-commerce and moving data back and forth between a Web browser and a database. There's xml.com, a resource site to learn, and stay current with, extensible markup language, often called the next generation language to power the Internet.

Each year, O'Reilly & Associates hosts several conferences, the biggest being the O'Reilly Open Source convention, where 2,000 people pow-wow over the direction and future of software that's written by a global community of developers.

The company's other conferences, on emerging technology and bioinformatics, attract 400 to 500 attendees. Gathering these customer communities together is a key part of O'Reilly's marketing strategy that provides the following benefits:

- A chance for O'Reilly's customers to meet other customers under the O'Reilly banner
- A forum for the company to understand which issues are important to its customers
- A chance to gather feedback and input on existing products and services

"Ideas grow in value as you spread them often," O'Reilly says. "People worry that they'll be totally ripped off . . . [but] you can tell people virtually anything and know you're safe. If somebody out-executes you, it's a good incentive to you."[26]

Much has been made of the future of e-Books and other computer-housed books whose promoters have said could mean big changes in paper-based publishing. While the major e-Book programs to date have failed to gain traction, O'Reilly partnered with six other technical publishers to launch the "Safari" online book program in 2001. Designed as a subscription service that puts the contents of its popular titles online, an entire manuscript is searchable; online tools allow the titles to be annotated and bookmarked. Like Napster, the company's digitized intellectual property has a streamlined and faster channel of distribution.

Is O'Reilly concerned about his company's intellectual property moving through cyberspace without traditional control structures in place?

"It certainly has to happen where we give away ideas and somebody comes along and does better with them, but I go, hey, it's part of the game. I once gave a talk at some publishing conference and the Border's buyer said, 'Well, you just gave all your competitors their program for the year.' I just go out and say here's what I think is interesting as opposed to I'm going to play my cards close to the vest. Somebody once said to me, 'The reason I like O'Reilly is because you don't have too many MBAs who have figured out that you're not doing it right.'"[27]

Lessons learned:

- When the heft of a competitive advantage is intellectual property, make it more valuable by offering reams of free supporting material.
- The march of Napsterization continues; subscription models for intellectual property are possible, and more so if they can be searched, annotated, and bookmarked.
- "Ideas grow in value as you spread them."

CUSTOMER FEEDBACK DRIVES PRODUCT IMPROVEMENT AND INNOVATION

The company gathers feedback through three primary channels: e-mail, trade shows, and its customer call center. O'Reilly says that gathering feedback at trade shows is "a virtuous circle because you're visible. You have people come to you. If you're not visible, you have to actually go out and solicit information."[28]

In 1986, before the World Wide Web was born, O'Reilly recognized the potential of e-mail as a customer feedback touchpoint. He included his e-mail address at the time—DECVAX!adelie!ora!tim—in books and encouraged readers to send him feedback.

> You have got to have a product that makes people feel attached. The virtuous cycle keeps going if people get what they expect. Build expectations. You have this great community market. People feel betrayed when you let them down. That's part of the customer dialogue. The most successful open source projects are those that have . . . effectively made an efficient market and status, where people get acknowledged a lot—they get this positive feedback loop. We've done a lot of the same thing by getting our customers involved, giving us ideas, being involved in contributing to our books, writing the books. When the products are available, we already have this group of people who are already invested.[29]

O'Reilly defines the need of customer involvement as a core component of the overall human experience. "If you give people some sense that they contribute, then it's like a gift," he says. "They want that. There's some sense in which customercentric marketing is letting people be part of something bigger. That whole impulse to say, 'I'm part of something big, I'm part of something successful, I'm part of some movement,' is a very natural human impulse. By getting our customers involved, giving us ideas, contributing to our books, writing the books, we have this set of people who are already invested when the products are available."[30]

One of O'Reilly's heroes is Harold, the last of the Saxon kings of England in 1066. Harold had promised William of Normandy—perhaps under duress—that he had no desire for the crown. Yet sure enough, Harold had been ordained king of England. An upset William was out for revenge and launched an attack in the southern part of Harold's kingdom. "Basically, all of Harold's advisors were saying—when William was raping and pillaging . . . in the south of England—take your time. Regroup. Get your troops together," O'Reilly explains. "Harold clucked, 'That's not the deal. These are my people.'"[31]

So Harold sped his exhausted troops south and met William in Yorkshire for the famous Battle of Hastings. Harold and his troops fought gallantly, knowing their lives and possibly the future of England was at stake. History asserts that had Harold let his southern kingdom die so that he and his troops could regroup, perhaps he and his troops would have defeated William.

O'Reilly says the story of Harold, the Saxon king, motivates his approach to customers. "I feel like we owe our customers something," O'Reilly says. "It's not just what we're selling them. If you want your customers to be loyal to you, you have to be loyal to them."[32]

Lessons learned:

- Collect customer feedback at every customer touch point.
- Allowing people to contribute feedback to your business lets them be part of something bigger than themselves.

EVANGELISM SCORECARD: O'REILLY & ASSOCIATES

Customer Plus-Delta

- Tim O'Reilly encourages readers to e-mail him directly with ideas and suggestions at letters.oreilly.com.

Napsterized Knowledge

- The company's Web site <www.oreilly.com> is a vast pool of information and knowledge that extends well beyond its published books.
- Safari Tech Books online brought together many technical book publishers to put book contents online as a subscription service <www.safari.oreilly.com>.

Build the Buzz

- The company features non-techie animal etchings on its covers.
- Tim O'Reilly uses the Web to extensively communicate issues to the community.
- A strong focus on relationships with bookstores resulted in the creation of O'Reilly bookstore "shrines."

Create Community

- The company invites evangelists into an exclusive evangelism community.
- The annual O'Reilly conferences bring customers together under the company's umbrella.
- O'Reilly's 35 different e-mail newsletters keep various communities in the loop on issues internal and external to the group.

Bite-Size Chunks

- Its expansive Web sites feature excerpts from books as well as updated information.

Create a Cause

- Tim O'Reilly campaigns on behalf of open-standards software and encourages the development of the open source movement.

Coordinates

Company:	O'Reilly & Associates
Headquarters:	Sebastopol, California
Founded:	1978
President:	Tim O'Reilly
Marketing chief:	Mark Brokering
Description:	Computer books / conferences / online publishing
Industry:	Publishing
Employees:	300
Ownership:	Privately held
Web site:	<www.oreilly.com>

CHAPTER 12

THE NEW MAVERICKS OF MARKETING

the dallas mavericks

"Treat every customer like a god. Gods will introduce you to other gods."[1]

—DALLAS MAVERICKS owner Mark Cuban

Mark Cuban is a rebel with a cause. He's out to make life better for long-suffering Dallas Mavericks fans. He wants to overthrow the egalitarianism of the NBA, introduce new levels of marketing sophistication to the sport, and bring fans closer to a game that has been declining in popularity since 1997.

Since purchasing the Mavericks in 2000 for $285 million ($200 million for the team and $85 million for part ownership of the arena), Cuban has helped revive a dormant franchise into a winning team—both on the court and in the back office. Take-it-or-leave-it fans have morphed into a raucous group that encouraged the team to reach the second round of the NBA playoffs in 2001 under coach Don Nelson. The last time the team had made the playoffs was in 1990. In 2002, the team had a record of 57–25 and made it to the second round of the playoffs.

Cuban is certainly the most visible and approachable professional sports team owner in the past 20 years. He attends every Mavericks game and sits courtside, cheering his team on and hollering at the referees. During home games in Dallas's American Airlines Center, the scoreboard flashes his e-mail address: mark.cuban@dallasmavs.com. He hosts his own television program, *The Mark Cuban Show*. After games, he's often seen in the arena's two-level bar, hobnobbing with hundreds of fans and downing dozens of Diet Cokes.

Cuban has a knack for converting missteps into marketing manna. As "The Dairy Queen Guy," he was the billionaire who stuck his size 11 foot in his mouth; his continuous complaints against the NBA's consistency in officiating culminated in an off-hand remark that he wouldn't hire the NBA's chief referee "to manage a Dairy Queen." As we recounted in an earlier chapter, what could have been a PR disaster turned into a stint of Cuban "managing" a Dallas-area Dairy Queen.[2]

Cuban's media-fueled ubiquity hasn't come without its critics. Sports writers have the most enmity for Cuban's invasion of what he calls "the NBA country club." *Dallas Morning News* columnist Kevin B. Blackistone summarizes the media's love-hate relationship this way: "He has played those of us in the media just as adroitly as he has played the NBA commish. He has had us turn him into arguably the most famous sports team owner in the country, right up there with George Steinbrenner and Jerry Jones, but for all the wrong reasons. Steinbrenner and Jones made their celebrity primarily by winning. Cuban is making his primarily by whining."[3]

The team's success on the court since Cuban took over in 2000 has certainly been a big part of renewed fanaticism and improved fortunes. In the 2000–2001 season, the team finished 53–29 and made it to the conference semifinals, with 20 of its regular season 41 home games sold out. In the 2001–2 season, the team sold out 34 of its 41 regular season home games.

Despite the Mavs' success on the court, it would be difficult to argue that Cuban's kinetic ownership and visibility have hurt the bottom line. Season ticket sales in 2001–2 were up 50 percent over the previous year, and merchandise sales increased more than tenfold. Sponsorship revenue increased 30 percent during the same period.

Forbes reports that the Mavs' valuation as a franchise for the 2000–2001 season increased 26 percent from the previous season. For the 2001–2 season, that increase rose to 35 percent. In February 2002 the business magazine ranked the franchise the 15th most valuable of the 29 in the NBA, pegging its total worth at $211 million, with annual revenues of $68 million. As an NBC-TV commentator said during a televised Mavericks playoff game in May 2001, "Thanks to the Mavericks and Mark Cuban, Dallas has become a basketball town." That's a feat, considering the Dallas Cowboys have commanded the majority of sports fans' attention in Dallas for decades.

A hallmark of a marketing evangelist is the ability to shepherd more believers into the flock. This is true whether one has the capability and fortitude to own a professional sports team or not; the lessons here are for medium-sized companies with high profile talent and visibility, especially in the entertainment industry, which is where Cuban says he competes.

The evidence shows that the entertainment value Cuban brings to the court is packing the pews with throngs of believers.

The Dallas Mavericks have created customer evangelists because:

- Owner Mark Cuban connects with customers.
- The team focuses on the customer "experience."
- The cause is bigger than a championship trophy.
- Its marketing strategy is responsive and flexible.

OWNER MARK CUBAN CONNECTS WITH CUSTOMERS

Mark Cuban is a bags-to-riches story. His roots are planted in Pittsburgh, Pennsylvania. The grandson of Russian immigrants, Cuban demonstrated an early entrepreneurial aptitude. At age 12, when Cuban asked his father for new basketball shoes, the elder Cuban challenged him to earn them. His father's poker buddy suggested selling garbage bags door-to-door in the South Hills neighborhood of Squirrel Hill.

"Who can say no to a kid selling garbage bags?" Cuban asks, recounting his first paying job at age 12. "No one said no. They were cheap-ass garbage bags for $6 a box, and I would go back once every couple of weeks and refill 'em. I had my little garbage bag route."

Other jobs included selling magazine subscriptions and greeting cards door-to-door and a stint as a box boy at a drugstore. "You name it, I've done it."[4]

He dropped out of Pittsburgh's Mount Lebanon High School, which oddly enough, didn't prevent him from enrolling at, and later graduating from, Indiana University with a business degree. At Indiana, his entrepreneurial ambition continued; he gave disco lessons and started a chain letter that paid for his junior year's tuition. He pooled his college financial aid with the money of friends and opened Motley's Pub in Bloomington, Indiana.

Cuban's penchant for challenging The System began at IU. During his freshman year, he enrolled in the business school's graduate courses because he thought they looked interesting. Today's more sophisticated computer-based college enrollment systems would prevent such an occurrence, but in the late 1970s Cuban took graduate-level courses in entrepreneurship, accounting, finance, and statistics. Wayne Winston taught the statistics class, and Cuban later recruited him to be his secret statistician to evaluate NBA referees' performances.

"By the time I was through with my sophomore year, I had a year and a half of my MBA done," Cuban says. Then the dean of the business school found out.

"I'll never forget; he starts poking his finger in my chest going, 'I don't know what the hell you did or how the hell you got away with it, but you are going back to undergrad. This is bullshit; you can't make a mockery of the school," Cuban remembers the dean telling him.[5]

Broke and unsure of his future after graduation, Cuban took up residence with six other guys in a three-bedroom Dallas apartment. He launched computer consultancy MicroSolutions without any backing. Cuban's sales charm helped him land customers even though he didn't know much about computers or programming. "Oh, you want that done in dBase? No problem," he says, explaining how he would close the sale and then cram all night learning how to program dBase.

Seven years later, MicroSolutions was grossing $30 million a year. He sold the company to CompuServe for $5 million and then played the stock market for about a year. One day in 1995, friend Todd Wagner wondered aloud, "Wouldn't it be great to listen to Indiana University basketball games over the Internet here in Dallas?"[6]

Thus, AudioNet—later renamed broadcast.com—was born, sowing the seeds of Cuban's eventual membership in the billionaire boys club; he and Wagner sold the company to Yahoo! for a reported $5.7 billion. Cuban's take: a reported $2 billion. Cuban was one of the few Internet pioneers who sold out before the tech bubble burst. If luck and timing were the names of an intersection, Cuban would own all of the surrounding property.

Now that he had pole-vaulted onto the lists of the richest Americans, Cuban considered his options. He set out to buy Napster, but Bertelsmann beat him out before he could finalize an offer. There was his passion for basketball—he was, after all, at Indiana during basketball coach Bobby Knight's heyday. Cuban met with then Mavericks owner Ross Perot, Jr., and through a series of meetings, Cuban, the expert salesman, sold Perot on the idea of selling the Mavericks. They announced the deal on January 4, 2000. Cuban says the purchase wasn't a business investment so much as a "decision of passion."

Rick Alm is a reporter at the *Dallas Morning News*. He has covered the high-dollar world of sports ownership since 1994. Alm says Cuban's formula for successful ownership has two ingredients: "passion and impatience."

"He's very focused on who his audience is," Alm says. "As you walk around town, you get a casual sense of his personal involvement. That's translated very well into the fans' opinion of him. And it helps that he has dramatically improved the team."[7]

After a game in Dallas one balmy night in January 2002 after the Mavs had just lost to the Los Angeles Clippers, we corraled a group of fans. Some of them were what the Mavericks call "Painted People," those who paint their faces and bodies in Mavs' regalia. We asked for their opinion of Cuban's work. (See Figure 12.1.)

"He's the man!" says Todd Walley, emphatically. Walley has painted his entire face in Mavericks blue. A pretty good rendering of the team's basketball-and-pony logo covers his bare belly. "He's the only team owner who comes down to games in blue jeans and T-shirts. He's not stuck up. He's one of us, you know?"[8]

Chris Bontrager painted his bare chest to resemble a Mavericks uniform. He has been a fan "ever since he can remember." Fandom was tough during the 1990s, Bontrager says. It's different now. "Cuban has brought the buzz back to Dallas for basketball," he says. "It's a complete 180. Everybody's excited about the team again."[9]

Besides his penchant for body paint, which he calls a fun outlet to "go out and get loose," Bontrager says he persistently lines up friends to attend games and generate enthusiasm for the team. "Oh yeah, I try to persuade them all the time," he says.

George Killebrew is the Mavericks' vice president of corporate sponsorship and a back-office veteran since 1991. He reports that fans compete for Cuban's attention with homemade signs as much as they compete for the attention of players.

"We used to have a rule in the old arena that you couldn't bring a sign in because it would obstruct someone's view," Killebrew says. "Is that what you really want if you're marketing entertainment and sports?"[10]

Cuban's personal involvement means many things. First among them: Do not behave like a royal owner, perched in a skybox with the rest of the well-heeled crowd. Although he usually sits near his team courtside during home games, Cuban joins fans in the $8 seats high above the court five to ten times a season. He chats with anyone who approaches him, devoid of handlers, obliging every request for an autograph or picture. This way, Cuban discovers what his customers like and love, loathe and hate.

When he took ownership of the team, the Mavs held a strong command over last place in its division. During the 1992–93 season, when Don Carter owned the team, the Mavs' record was 11–71, two games shy of tying a terrible NBA record. On his first day as the new owner, Cuban called season ticket holders on the phone and asked them to hang in there, promising that improvements would be coming soon.

To create what he calls "a fresh look for a fresh start," Cuban updated the team's logo and uniforms, which hadn't been updated in the team's 21-

Figure 12.1 | **Dallas Mavericks' Painted People Fans**

The Dallas Mavericks encourage its most rambunctious fans to become "Painted People," who often go all out in wearing the team's colors. Painted People fans are often given good seats, courtesy of the team.

year history. The change process normally takes a full year, but Cuban and his back office team changed the logo, all marketing materials, and uniforms between seasons.

"That's a good example of his impatience and desire to get things done," Alm says "Not any of the other owners would have done it like that."[11]

Nor would many owners have introduced the new uniforms using a fashion show motif, complete with a runway. Cuban did, using two of the players as models.

Nor do most team owners personally market the products of their other customers—the team sponsors. Cuban does. He advocates and appears in ads for Body Solutions, a weight-loss product, and Planet Tan, a tanning company.

"He'll always go the extra mile for his sponsors," Alm says.[12]

During the 2000–2001 playoffs, the team offered free admission to fans who painted their faces in the team's colors. The next season, the Mavs launched its Painted People section as a full-scale, season-long program supported by a corporate sponsor. Painted People cheer 30 rows up from the floor in a section where seats typically cost $51 each.

Then there's *The Mark Cuban Show*. The team's local television partner pitched the idea and "upped their offer for the Mavs TV package if I did,"[13] Cuban says. Once a week, Cuban hosts a 30-minute . . . how shall we describe this . . . variety show. He promotes the players, coaches, ticket packages, himself, and the Mavericks dancers. Tapings are held at a local watering hole and are open to the public. At a January 2002 taping, Cuban works the room before, during, and after the show. He has a smile, a wave, a finger point for everyone who catches his attention. Coach Don Nelson is that night's guest. On the air, Cuban asks him to recall their first meeting.

"I thought you were probably going to let me go," Nelson says.

"Were you having fun at that point?" Cuban asks.

Nelson laughs. "No, I wasn't."

"Are you having fun now?" Cuban asks.

Nelson smiles. "Hell yes," he answers.

Lessons learned:

- Be accessible to your customers, especially the fans who seek you out.
- Help your customers succeed with their businesses.
- Offer your most devoted fans—your evangelists—incentives for connecting with you at an even deeper level.

THE TEAM'S FOCUS ON THE CUSTOMER EXPERIENCE

Cuban wants fans to know his e-mail address—in case you missed it earlier, it's mark.cuban@dallasmavs.com. Every day, about 1,000 e-mails fill Cuban's computer screen, and he contends he answers every one unless it asks for money or a job. A nightmare or dream screen? Cuban loves it. It's a well of ideas.

An e-mail, for example, arrived one day in 2001 from a fan who had attended a game but had trouble seeing the 24-second shot clock perched above the basketball net's glass backboard. The clock was designed for players to see, not necessarily fans. How about a three-sided shot clock so everyone in the arena could see, the fan suggested. Several weeks and $24,000 later, brand-new, three-sided shot clocks were perched above the backboards of each basket. Most of the NBA has since adopted the idea.

Fans were telling Cuban they had trouble getting to the arena's box office. A twisty maze of roads off Stemmons Expressway southwest of downtown Dallas leading to the arena box office can be confusing even for locals. The team responded by opening a satellite ticket office downtown with easy parking.

"Rule number one of any business is listen to your customers," Cuban says.[14] Other ideas from fans that have become Cuban action items: fixing broken seats, improving the signage in the arena's parking lot, ensuring that hot dogs are hotter and beer is colder, and stopping fans from trudging up and down the aisles while the ball is in play.

More evidence that basketball is more entertainment than sporting event is the way Cuban coaches his sales team to sell an experience and entertainment, not a win-loss record. He argues that people who attend a sporting event "don't remember how many passes were thrown. You might remember something that was artistic—a big dunk, a great run, a homerun, or a throw—but you remember how you felt," Cuban says. "The things you remember are what you felt inside, and that's what we sell. The thing I spend the most time on is trying to work on the experience in the arena. That's what I focus on the most because that's where I control my own destiny. It's all about the game experience because it's like throwing a party every night. You can't run out of beer at a party."[15]

Having owned a bar during his college days, Cuban should know. During home games, Cuban often dashes from his seat to the scorekeeper's desk. He says it's to keep the arena video and audio technicians who mix in music, sound effects, video snippets, and prerecorded cheers alert to each event associated with the game. In fact, he usually recommends specific music and video selections.

"You might see me mad at the refs, but you'll see me madder if it's a critical part of the game and they're not playing 'Let's go Mavs' or 'Defense,'" Cuban says. "You'll see me stand up and run over to those people and say 'Get it going!'"[16]

By dedicating resources and energy to the overall experience, not just the players on the court, Cuban and his substantive back-office team say they can do their jobs better.

"It matters not who our opponent is or what our record is, whether it's against the [Los Angeles] Clippers on a Tuesday night or the [Los Angeles] Lakers on a Saturday night," says George Prokos, the team's director of new revenue. "Bottom line: there's no excuse why we don't fill the building every night."[17]

The customer experience at American Airlines Center often extends beyond basketball. The team has booked live music performances to immediately follow some games. In 2001, a postgame performance by country music crooner Pat Green helped fill 6,000 unsold seats. The concert strategy worked well during the 2000–2001 season, when six concerts brought in $50,000 to $80,000 each. Even though the team broke even on the effort, the bigger strategy was to bring in more people to experience the spectacle of a modern-day basketball/entertainment extravaganza.

The team creates bite-size chunks of its season ticket program by allowing fans to purchase five-game or ten-game ticket packets. During the 2000–2001 season, the team sold 7,000 "mini-plans," as they are called. Thirty percent of the plan purchasers upgraded to a half-season program and 25 percent upgraded to a full season.

Lessons learned:

- When customers complain that something is broken, fix it!
- Your best opportunity to create evangelists is a positive, memorable experience.
- Make it easy and inexpensive for customers to sample your most expensive offering.

WHY THE CAUSE IS BIGGER THAN A CHAMPIONSHIP TROPHY

At the onset of his ownership, Cuban gave his team a goal of making it to the playoffs within two years. It worked. They made it in one. He also added 30 additional salespeople to an existing staff of 5. There were 4,800 season ticket holders when Cuban bought the team; two years later, that number quadrupled to over 16,000. Like any successful leader, he executed his strategy every day using incentives and enthusiasm, not fear and intimidation.

Cuban capitalized on the team's underdog status. He played up his role as a "fan-based owner," the outsider who's just a fan at heart. It seems the team's players connect with their boss, too. At 7'6", center Shawn Bradley is the team's tallest player and also one of its veterans. He's been a Maverick sine 1997, three years before Cuban bought the team. What's different now?

"The team mood is one of confidence," Bradley says in April 2002, just before the team was readying for the playoffs for the second time in two years. "The Perots were great owners and wonderful people, and I think everyone on the team liked them, but they approached the team from a real business aspect.

"Cuban does that too, but he also adds an element of confidence and player support that is unique to any team that I have been on." [18]

Says teammate Greg Buckner, who was also with the team prior to Cuban, "On the basketball side of things, he has made a complete turnaround." [19]

Cuban defines his cause as excellence and fun. "I want to have fun, I want to be the best, and I want to make a lot of money doing it. It's that simple." [20] Actually, it's a bit deeper than that. Continuing in his tradition of challenging The System, Cuban says his role is not to please NBA commissioner David Stern, who has fined him more than $1 million for speaking out. (It's more than $2 million if one factors in that Cuban matches each fine with a donation to charity.) Cuban's larger cause is making the NBA exciting and entertaining again. Average attendance at NBA games has been in decline since 1997, when 17,135 fans attended each game. During the 2000–2001 season, that number was 16,778. That same season, Dallas jumped from 11th to 8th in attendance, with average attendance at 16,589.

Cuban's whistle crisis with NBA officiating is a smaller part of his cause. Deeper still, Cuban considers corporate culture a root problem of what troubles the league.

"You have to set the culture because that's how people make decisions," he says. "If you don't know what your cause is, if you don't know what your culture is and what you're rewarded for and what's respected and what's expected, then you'll make mistakes when you let people make judgments. Then you get all kinds of autocratic environments that don't succeed." [21]

The team burrows its roots into the community as deeply as possible. The team's summer "hoop camp" attracts 2,500 kids. The nonprofit Dallas

Mavericks Foundation supports charitable causes in the Dallas-Fort Worth area. In 2001, it donated $1 million in cash gifts and in-kind donations.

For the team's most passionate fans, there is the Mavs Fan For Life VIP Club, called MFFL for short (Cuban says it's another idea borrowed from a fan's e-mail). This loyalty program's $35 entrance fee is good for team merchandise, a player's autographed picture, and perhaps, most appealingly, the chance to meet players and coaches in person after a game. The team launched the MFFL program during the 2001–2 season; a few months later, 500 members were in the program.

Lessons learned:

- When sales are declining, improve the product/service quickly.
- Create reward-based incentives for your team, not fear-based punishment.
- For your biggest fans and evangelists, provide an opportunity to join your cause—people want to belong to something that's bigger than themselves.

A RESPONSIVE AND FLEXIBLE MARKETING STRATEGY

Matt Fitzgerald is responsible for all of the Mavs' marketing and communications. A former senior marketing manager at Coca-Cola Company, Fitzgerald first met Cuban in 1999 playing basketball at a Dallas gym. Over the course of their weekly basketball diaries, Fitzgerald asked Cuban if he should accept a promotion Coke was offering. Cuban told him to instead consider working with the Mavericks. During a meeting in which Fitzgerald presented a formal "Restaging the Mavericks" plan, Cuban offered this sports industry outsider the job of chief marketing Maverick.

"Instead of selecting a marketing person from the NBA or the sports industry, Mark consciously made a decision to hire someone from outside the industry," Fitzgerald says. "He believed the NBA marketing community was too in-bred so [Cuban] was looking for a marketing person with a fresh perspective and ideas." [22]

Like his billionaire boss, Fitzgerald focuses on customer communications to build and maintain goodwill. "We answer every e-mail that comes in. The whole organization answers e-mail." [23]

In an e-mail to Cuban in January 2002, a fan suggested a promotion to capitalize on all-star forward Dirk Nowitzki's recent and impromptu head-shaving. During warm-ups before a game, Nowitzki had dashed into the locker room to have his head completely shorn of its ample blond locks.

Cuban forwarded the fan's idea to Fitzgerald, who was happy to report they were already building a plan.

A few weeks later, the team launched a promotion for fans to shave their heads for charity—in this case, breast cancer research and treatment. Held on the night the Mavs played the Los Angeles Clippers, 75 fans lined up to get their heads shaved in exchange for a free ticket. The idea landed ProCuts as a corporate sponsor to join the team's existing roster of 100 other sponsors. So fastidious is the team's awareness about the marketing allure of its players that a team employee scooped up all of Nowitzki's shorn hair from the locker room floor and auctioned it for charity, Fitzgerald says.

This move-fast mentality is based on what Fitzgerald calls "real-time feedback." "We don't subscribe to a lot of the traditional types of research —focus groups—because we see this arena as a giant focus group every night," he says. "We're not afraid to try things. Quite frankly, a lot of things we do don't work but it's OK because we just move on. It's all about doing a lot of little things."[24]

After the Mavs had lost two key games against the Utah Jazz in the 2001 playoffs, Cuban told his back-office team that he would purchase up to 2,000 tickets for fans to attend the next game in Salt Lake City. The catch: fans had to find their own way to Utah and paint their faces in Mavs' colors. The next morning, Fitzgerald and his team flooded Ticketmaster's phone lines, scooping up 680 tickets. The team announced the promotion on its Web site, and in 45 minutes 1,500 fans were ready to make the trip. In Salt Lake City, Fitzgerald gathered the fans at a hotel across from the arena, threw a party, and guided them to surround the team's bus as it arrived, cheering the players on into the arena.

Did it work? The Mavs came back from being 17 points down in the third quarter to win the game and advance to the second round of the playoffs.

"It's just rapid-fire," Fitzgerald says of their marketing approach. "For a sports team, it's really buzz marketing that works best. It's [Cuban's] style, and it works really well for us."[25] The way it works: every day Cuban filters his e-mail for ideas. He forwards the ideas he likes or the complaints that should be heard to the appropriate department head, usually with a brief action comment.

"You know how a lot of organizations behave where everybody is filtering up to the top?" Fitzgerald asks. "Here, it's the inverse. Everything comes through him, and he filters it out to the organization. The momentum swings so quickly. You have to be very flexible and ready to just jump on things when they become available."

Fitzgerald says the flexibility comes from not having an ironclad marketing budget and plan.

"We're a completely idea-driven organization," he says. "If there's an idea to have a fun party to get people going, we do it. That's not to say that Mark funds every idea.

"In the world I came from, there was a lot of vacillation back and forth—should we do it, shouldn't we do it. With Mark, it's just an e-mail away. He could say, 'That's stupid, that sucks, no way.' Or he could say, 'I love it. Go ahead and do it.' We just move. We move. We move. We move."[26]

Cuban keeps things moving by demanding weekly e-mail reports from his back-office team.

"And the bad news has to go first," Cuban says. "For a salesperson, if they're losing a customer, boom! I want to see the customer we lost because that's the trigger item. I'm always looking for the trigger item, what's going on that I need to understand."[27]

To keep his marketing and sales efforts responsive, Cuban says that "you'll never see me do branding, ever. I'm a big believer that you go for the call to action and that if you're providing value and you let people know about the value, then your marketing takes care of itself." That also means no meetings.

"I am Mr. Anti-Meeting," he says. "I hate meetings. Everybody postures. You create a report, and you're just going to read it to me. Just send it to me and I can read it sitting on the toilet in the morning."[28]

Cuban's 30 salespeople also rely heavily on fans for referrals and help. "You'd better be asking for referrals in everything you do," Cuban says. "The underpinning is that you treat every customer like a god. Gods will introduce you to other gods.

"Being a good company is like being a good lover: First you ask your partner what they want, then you give it to them. Then you ask them if they liked it. If they say yes, you give it to them again! That's what customer service is all about: being good to people. If someone enjoys the experience, it makes them look good to tell somebody else. If you focus on one, it leads to the other."[29]

Asked if he has transferred the idea of marketing on "Internet time"— a reference to the instant communications approach prevalent on the World Wide Web—to the Mavericks, Cuban replies: "It's about customers' time. We all live in a world where everything happens in real time. You have to move at the speed that your competitors are moving. There's always a new movie, there's always a new restaurant, there's always a new opportunity. That's my competition. If I don't move, then I'm going to lose."[30]

Competition for entertainment dollars—where Cuban says he competes —is fierce. To succeed, he says he must continually focus on increasing the average lifetime value of a Mavs season ticket holder. In 2002, that figure was $300,000, according to Cuban. "The [Chicago] Cubs, you've got to wait in line to get your season tickets," he says. "That's the goal . . . then I don't have to spend lots of money on salespeople and all kinds of support efforts—I've just got to keep [customers] happy. It's a lot easier to keep 'em happy than to go out and get new ones to replace 'em."[31]

The Mavericks' marketing is not just for fans and corporate sponsors; the team also markets itself to players on other teams. After all, with the realities of midseason trades and free agency, today's most reviled opponent could be tomorrow's star forward. In the visitors' locker room at American Airlines Center, the settings are roomy and luxurious. For a while, visiting players were given their own towels and robes, free for the taking. But the NBA put a stop to that during the 2001–2 season.

The Mavericks' locker room resembles an expensive health club: beautiful wood, carpet, pool table, leather couches. Game films are viewed on large, high-definition televisions. A weight room rivals those found at large, downtown gyms. Each player's locker comes equipped with a flat-screen TV, a CD/DVD player, stereo system, and a Sony Playstation 2.

Surprised that the team was viewing game films by threading actual film into a projector, Cuban commissioned a system to digitize the films and make them viewable on PCs. This allows coaches and players to study opposing teams' games on their laptops while at home, traveling, in the whirlpool, wherever.

The word is out.

"Just recently I heard a few of the other NBA players talking about how this is the place that other players want to come and play for," Shawn Bradley says. "Some players want to be a Dallas Maverick because of the environment and the situation that Cuban has created here."[32]

The Mavs' Greg Buckner says Cuban's work has "set the standard for other owners in the NBA. Other teams are now trying to match what he has done and what he continues to do so they can compete in the free agent market."[33]

The team's investment in technology extends to tickets, too. A common problem for many sports teams is sellouts that aren't sellouts. Scores of empty seats often belie announced attendance figures. At each home game, every used ticket is scanned for a unique bar code that tells the back-office team who attended and who didn't. The next day the team calls a ticket owner to say, "Hey, we missed you last night," Prokos says. "Is there something we can do to enhance the experience to help ensure you use those tickets?"[34] Although declining to divulge specific numbers in what they call their "drop count," Prokos says the effort has a "marked difference" for improving attendance.

Finally, there is the January 2002 Dairy Queen incident. Both organizations skillfully turned a verbal slam into a marketing slam dunk. Now when an opposing player or coach is ejected from a game, they are "DQ'd," much to the delight of new sponsor Dairy Queen. "Part of the point I was trying to make with the NBA is that you have to understand your customers and learn to get better as a business," Cuban says.[35] Did it help the NBA? Perhaps.

Did it help the Mavericks and Dairy Queen sell more stuff? Hell, yeah. Lessons learned:

- Customer feedback delivered from the top down rather than from the bottom up results in a more customer-responsive organization.
- The only "time" to live on is "customer time"—respond at the rate customers require or faster.
- Marketing yourself to your competitors can make you more attractive to future employees.
- Understand how many customers are a no-show and ask them why.

EVANGELISM SCORECORD: DALLAS MAVERICKS

Customer Plus-Delta

- Cuban encourages fans to send him e-mail. Many contain suggestions for improvement.
- The Mavericks' Web site has a bulletin board filled with thousands of comments.

Napsterize Your Knowledge

- "The more you try to hide information, obviously the more things you have to hide," Cuban says.
- Cuban publishes a customer e-mail every day as a continuously growing FAQ (frequently asked questions) source.

Build the Buzz

- Cuban publicly voices NBA issues to generate discussion.

- The team's marketing group capitalizes on fast-moving opportunities —the Dairy Queen incident and Dirk Nowitzki's shaving his head, for examples.

Create Community

- The team encourages fans to talk about the team and with one another <www.dallasmavericks.com>.
- By encouraging and rewarding fans for decorating themselves in the team's colors and logo, the team engenders a deeper bond with fans.
- Dallas Mavericks Foundation Community service (Hoops for Hearts program with the American Hospital Association).

Bite-Size Chunks

- The team offers five-game and ten-game ticket packets as an introduction to full-season ticket ownership.

Create a Cause

- Cuban publicly lobbies for changes in the NBA's strategies and tactics.
- The team created a loyalty program called Mavs Fan For Life VIP Club available to any fan.

Coordinates

Company:	Dallas Mavericks
Headquarters:	Dallas, Texas
Owner:	Mark Cuban
Marketing chief:	Matt Fitzgerald
Description:	NBA franchise/professional sports team
Industry:	Sports
Employees:	110
Ownership:	Privately held
Web site:	<www.dallasmavericks.com>

CHAPTER 13

A BEAR MARKET FOR RETAILING
build-a-bear workshop

"Every single one of our customers is engaged in the process

of making Build-A-Bear Workshop more famous

by telling someone about their experience." [1]

—MAXINE CLARK, founder and chief executive bear of Build-A-Bear Workshop

The retail industry has been lost in the woods for the past several years.

Montgomery Ward, initiator of the mail-order catalog, retail visionary, and inventor of the catchphrase "satisfaction guaranteed or your money back," filed for bankruptcy and closed for good. Born in 1872, it died in 2000.

Kmart, pioneer of discount retailing that began life as Kresge's, filed for bankruptcy in 2002 and announced it was closing 284 of its 2,114 stores. More than 22,000 employees were fired. Born in 1899, Kmart was on life support in 2002.

Pundits say the reasons for the downturn in retailing range from consistently poor customer service, miscalculated growth strategies, or too much supply with not enough demand. True, there's a lot more retail space in 2002 than in 1997.[2] Research by U.S. Bancorp Piper Jaffray reports that from 1998 through the end of 2000, retailers added nearly 1 trillion square feet of new store space to the American retail landscape. Yet retail profit margins had already been slipping from an industry average of 4 percent in 1996 to –.01 percent by the end of 2000.

Satisfaction among retail customers hasn't been setting any world records. The American Customer Satisfaction Index, which is compiled by the University of Michigan, shows that the retail industry has never surpassed a baseline satisfaction score set in 1994.

With this gloomy assessment, what's a retailer to do?

Maxine Clark has a pretty good idea. In 1997, she founded Build-A-Bear Workshop, a St. Louis–based retailer of stuffed animals. First-year revenues were $377,600. Four years later, Build-A-Bear has grown to 75 stores and over $100 million in revenues. A Build-A-Bear store rings up about $700 per square foot; the national mall average is $350.[3]

But the 4'11" Clark is no brash newcomer to the industry. As president and chief merchandiser of Payless Shoe Source from 1992 through 1996, she gave that retailer legs: She increased annual revenues from $1.5 billion in '92 to $2.3 billion by '96 and oversaw a network of 4,500 stores with 24,000 employees. Payless became the number one seller of kids' shoes in the world. During her presidency, one out of six pairs of shoes bought in the United States were from Payless.[4] As a decades-long executive of The May Department Stores Company (the parent company of Payless as well as Foley's and Lord & Taylor, among others), Clark understood retail as well as anyone. But something was missing.

Theater. Emotion. Connection.

"With Build-A-Bear Workshop, I am trying to go back to the way businesses used to be when they really focused on the customer from a personal perspective," Clark says.[5]

Childhood shopping memories resonate strongly with Clark, who turned 54 in 2002. Her mother, Anne, would take Maxine and sister Sharon on an hour-long trip to shop in downtown Miami. In the early to mid-1950s, shopping was an event, Clark says some 50 years later.

"We used to window-shop for entertainment," Clark says. "We would get dressed up—even wear hats and gloves sometimes. We would have lunch downtown, and it was special. The stores always had something going on."[6]

One store that forever captured Clark's imagination was Burdines. William Burdine opened his Miami general store in 1898; 104 years and 52 stores later, it's called "the store of Florida" because it has never expanded beyond its home state. In the 1950s, a rooftop circus was a big draw for Burdines. An attached gift store called the Little Shop was for kids to buy presents for their siblings. "Everything was really low—you could reach it— it was all done kind of like Santa's toyland," Clark says. "I have never forgotten that in my entire life, and it's the standard by which I measure everything that I do."[7]

Her turn-back-the-clock approach is propelling her forward. Clark won the 2001 Retail Innovator of the Year award from the Center for Retailing Studies at Texas A&M University. She was presented with the 1999 award for Emerging Entrepreneur of the Year from Ernst & Young. Her forward motion is helping shape the privately held Build-A-Bear Workshop into a global concern; its first store outside the United States opened in Great Britain in 2002.

Build-A-Bear Workshop creates customer evangelists because:

- The company focuses on a memorable experience.
- Customer feedback drives the business.
- Buying a product means joining a community.
- Its event-driven marketing is fast and responsive.

THE COMPANY'S FOCUS ON A MEMORABLE EXPERIENCE

What's wrong with retailing today?

Clark says retail stores are too boring, too predictable, and, worst of all, too forgettable.

After getting her journalism degree from the University of Georgia, Clark opted for the executive training program at the May Company instead of cub reporting at a newspaper. Starting out at Hecht's department stores, Clark rose through the ranks as an expert merchandiser. One of her more memorable assignments was to create a department for kids. She created a gift shop for kids called "The Land of Ahhs," just like the Little Shop Clark had remembered as a young girl on the roof of Burdines. "It was really well received, and I had a lot of fun doing it, but most of the time there's just not enough room in a department store to create that type of environment," Clark says.

Twenty-five years later, Clark said she was "bored with shopping." The words of her late mentor, the May Company's chairman Stanley Goodman, rang in her ear: "When customers have fun, they spend more money."[8]

Financially secure from her success, Clark quit without a clear plan. Although Payless went public a year later and with it the chance to build additional wealth, Clark says she has "no regrets." Besides, the entrepreneurial bug had bitten, and she wanted plenty of time and room to figure out her next move. She investigated buying a Krispy Kreme (see Chapter 9) franchise for St. Louis, but that effort didn't pan out.

Her research took her to a toy factory in China in 1996. Although she doesn't remember its name "because it was in Chinese," the factory offered tours to schools, so Clark says she tagged along on one. "When I went on the tour, I saw a special look in the children's eyes that said this idea had more potential," she says.[9]

The potential was to reinvent the concept of toy manufacturing inside a mall-based store. With $750,000 of her savings, Clark opened the first Build-A-Bear Workshop in the St. Louis Galleria in October 1997. Venture capitalists have supplied an additional $12 million.

A visit to a Build-A-Bear Workshop store is unlike a trip to most other retail stores, much less one that caters primarily to children and 'tweens, that group of kids between 9 and 12.

This is no Toys 'R' Us. A Build-A-Bear Workshop store averages 3,000 square feet, about the size of the average Gap location. There are no chattering robots, toy guns, or Barbies—just dozens upon dozens of unstuffed animals ($10–$25) lining the brightly colored walls with a few hundred outfits ($3–$15) resembling teeny baby clothes, ready for outfitting. Once a customer has decided on a favorite "skin," as the store associates call them, it's time to begin the 30-minute, life-giving process to the customer's new creation.

Working with a store associate whose official title is Master Bear Builder, customers fill the bears' skins using a boisterous stuffing machine

Figure 13.1 | **Build-A-Bear Workshop**

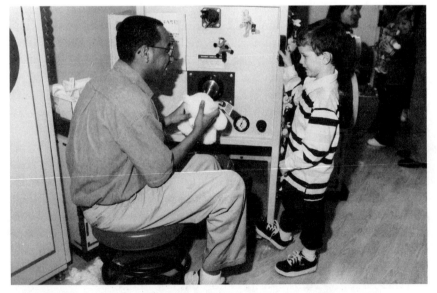

Children participate in the manufacturing of their own toys at Build-A-Bear Workshop.

that resembles a large movie theater popcorn maker. Customers select a soft and tiny red heart, personalize it with a wish and a kiss, and stuff it in with the stuffing.

This high-touch experience is high-tech, too. Customers can select a prerecorded voice to go on a computer chip inside each toy or record their own voice. (Customers who create a toy on the company's Web site can record their own voice over the telephone.) A unique bar code inside each toy identifies its owner in case child and toy are separated. People who find a misplaced teddy bear are encouraged to send it to Build-A-Bear Workshop, which routes it to the registered owner. Since the company began this lost-and-found program, more than 1,000 lost toys have been returned to their owners. Lost bears have been found on highways, at stadiums, in hotels, and, of course, at a store's mall.

Customers give their furry new friends a good brushing and a "bath" in a bathtublike area. Instead of water, streams of noisy air gush out of several spigots.

Bear birth is not an anonymous experience in the retail woods; customers are directed to a bank of computers to create a personalized birth certificate signed by Clark. The company captures each customer's name, gender, birthday, and street and e-mail address; about 90 percent of all customers register. This step in the store experience is smartly placed away from cash registers, where customers are usually in exit mode. A "birth certificate" commemorating the purchase is printed, and all of the data are sent to Build-A-Bear Workshop's central database, which remembers to send customers yearly birthday reminders, surveys, and newsletters.

With their information stored away now in the company's computers, customers proceed to the final stopping point: toy clothes. Part of the Build-A-Bear Workshop experience is the attention paid to product details, especially accessories; sneakers, for example, have real treads. The "bear binoculars" actually magnify distant objects; and pockets and purses are sewn to hold additional accessories.

Instead of a traditional shopping bag, customers tote their purchases in a "cub condo," a house-shaped box whose inspiration was the bagel container from Einstein's bagels. Every thing and every process has a name, usually derived from the word *bear*. The company is a universe of puns.

After five years of business, Build-A-Bear Workshop had registered 4 million customers and sold a total of 10 million toys, Clark reports. From the data it collects, the company knows how often its best customers purchase toys and how many they purchase.

Even more important, Clark's strategy of involving customers in the creation of their purchases results in their remembering the experience vividly and telling other people. "Every single one of our customers is engaged in the process of making Build-A-Bear Workshop more famous by telling some-one about the experience," Clark says, adding that "most" new customers heard about the store from a friend or family member. "The bulls-eye of our business is 11-year-old girls," Clark says. "Along with 11-year-old girls come 8-year-old brothers and their mothers and 13-year-old sisters. They are our evangelists because they are bringing a lot of people with them."[10]

Customer evangelists bring new customers into Build-A-Bear Workshop stores because of the many details that add up to a memorable store experience, Clark says. It's her strategic advantage and one that too many retailers ignore. Seemingly small, inconsequential details often derail memorable experiences. Ask Clark what she means and her characteristic candor comes out in full bear claw.

First, there's the always concerning problem of "nasty bathrooms." She's a bathroom inspector and says stores disrespect customers by not maintain-ing them. Then there are fitting rooms, most of which are cramped and poorly maintained, often filled with pins and detritus. Many customers, es-pecially women with children, avoid these messy, unsafe rooms, Clark adds. They would rather buy clothes, take them home to try on, and bring them back for exchanges and refunds rather than use a dressing room.

"If a company looked at how many people brought stuff home and brought it back . . . [they'd find] it's way more expensive to handle those transactions than [ensuring that customers] feel comfortable going into a fitting room and trying it on because the fitting room has appropriate mir-rors and space," Clark contends.[11]

Another problem is too many markdowns. Retailers today have be-come addicted to sales, which teach customers to visit your store only when markdowns occur, and that usually just devalues products and everything around them.

"I don't know of any department store in my area that doesn't have a sale going on every single week," Clark says, scoffing at the practice many retailers use to meet revenue targets.[12]

Because Build-A-Bear Workshop doesn't do markdowns, it relies on memorable experiences to create loyal customers, who visit an average of five times a year. The compensation of store managers is tied to customer satisfaction ratings. Each week, managers are notified of customer satisfac-tion scores, which are posted for all employees to see. Stores must meet minimum satisfaction goals to qualify for bonuses.

"These results are as important as our weekly sales," Clark says.[13]

By focusing on memorable experiences as its customer evangelism strategy rather than low prices or markdowns, Build-A-Bear Workshop en-hances its long-term value, an idea advocated by the National Quality Research Center at the University of Michigan Business School.

"Customer satisfaction based on low price is often fragile and highly dependent on the company's cost structure and price concessions from suppliers," according to Claes Fornell, the center's director.[14]

When asked what the big, nuts-and-bolts retailers can learn from her fast-growing success with Build-A-Bear Workshop, Clark says, "I don't care whether you make screws or sell screws, or you sell clothing . . . there's nothing a store can't do to improve its business. [Stores] can use more entertainment techniques, which are sitting right there in front of them. They just don't use them."

Lessons learned:

- "People buy more when they're having fun."
- The experience is part of the sale; a memorable experience creates buzz.
- Markdowns merely devalue the products sold and lessen the value of surrounding products.

CUSTOMER FEEDBACK DRIVES THE BUSINESS

Because Build-A-Bear Workshop's primary audience is e-mail savvy, the company relies heavily on electronic communications. So Clark's e-mail inbox fills up with 4,000 notes a month, most of them from customers.

A wire-bound volume of 175 customer e-mail printouts received during a several-month period in 2001 tells several stories.

- Most customers who had driven hours from their home just to visit a Build-A-Bear Workshop store ask for a store closer to their home— some even suggest specific locations.
- Customers describe their personal Build-A-Bear Workshop evangelism efforts, often including names of friends and family as well as descriptions of what they've said.
- Customer's report a high level of satisfaction with store employees— at least 75 percent of the e-mails name a specific employee who made a customer's experience memorable.

Clark says that every e-mail writer receives a personal response from her or one of the company's executive team. Responding to customer e-mail is not a "bear." In fact, she recommends that every executive team in the world do the same.

"I would absolutely recommend it 100 percent," Clark says. "I've had people tell me they think it's low-level, that they have a person who gets paid to do that. This is my monster. I go through life telling people this because I know I have not been listened to. I think companies have such bad habits from having secretaries read letters and handle customer problems."[15]

The company eschews administrative assistants, so Clark's management team is responsible for all of its own communications. That was a bit of a culture shock for Teresa Kroll, the company's "chief marketing bear," who left the May Company to join Build-A-Bear Workshop in 2001. "Obviously, you're thinking we can certainly afford secretaries," Kroll says, laughing. "But with the electronic exposure that we have today, we can get so many things done so much more quickly [by ourselves]."[16]

Several dozen kids keep Clark updated on their school activities, the health of their bears, and their life as children with daily or weekly e-mail updates. For Clark, this is like having her own personal research lab. "They are what I call Build-A-Bear Workshop fanatics," she says. "They are very much into Build-A-Bear. They are very much into the fact that they can write to me, and I respond back to them because I care. That's my interest. Their voice is important."[17]

Those voices have created 99 percent of the company's new products, according to Clark. One customer suggestion was to add a black Labrador as a product. The company did, and in its first six months, it sold 100,000 units. The company had already been offering shoes to go with each animal. Why not add socks? a customer suggested; shortly thereafter, the company did. Another customer suggested party rooms for birthdays and get-togethers, which the company began to offer in selected stores in 2002.

The company bolsters its feedback program with weekly surveys sent to customers, asking them to grade their store experience. It seems like a simple premise to ask a lot of customers every week or month to grade your performance. Why don't more retailers do that?

"I think everyone thinks they know who their customer is," Clark says. "They've been doing it the same way for such a long time. I was part of a very successful department store company for nearly 28 years of my retail life, and we didn't know half of what I know about my customers at Build-A-Bear Workshop.

"Those things drive me to think differently about my customer."[18]

Clark calls herself a quintessential shopper. She says it's not uncommon to find her trolling the aisles of dozens of stores after work and on the weekends, buying and researching merchandising trends. OK, a lot of buying. "My husband will tell you that I have a basement full of clothes with hang tags on them."[19]

As a result, she fills out six to seven customer surveys a year, always including her name and phone number, and then . . . nothing.

"No one has ever, ever called me on the phone and said, 'Thank you for taking the time to fill out our survey, and we hear what you are saying; we'd like to find out more details about it,'" Clark says, imagining what a store executive should be saying. "That little difference can make a huge amount of difference to a store's entertainment value and not entertainment because somebody put a piano player in the shoe department."[20]

When she was a young girl, Clark herself sat on the advisory board of a department store. Her turn-back-the-clock approach led her to launch Build-A-Bear Workshop's Cub Advisory Board, a group of 20 boys and girls 8 through 17 years old who review and suggest new products. It meets with Clark and her team three or four times a year to ensure that her stores are meeting the needs of her young and influential customers.

"Their candor has driven a number of product decisions and ideas," Clark says. "They are fearless and honest. They are also far more experienced shoppers [than previous generations] and selective about how they will spend their money.

"If they approve of something, we are pretty certain to have a winner."[21]

Lessons learned:

- Customer suggestions can speed up product development cycles and reduce research costs.
- Formalize customer input with a customer advisory board.
- Tie employee pay and/or bonuses to frequent customer satisfaction scores.

BUYING A PRODUCT MEANS JOINING A COMMUNITY

Clark says she retired from corporate life because it became "more about meetings and markdowns" and less about customers and creativity. She decided that any new venture "would have to play to my personal interests of inclusion rather than exclusion." To her, that means a heart-based community.

"Having a heart is more than a company strategy," Clark says. "It's a way of doing business. It extends to how people are treated in every aspect of the business. It is what excellent companies know is the core to success: treating vendors like partners, treating customers like guests, treating employees like friends and family.

"These characteristics and values are harder to find in today's fast-paced, hard-driving business world. We're not inventing anything new; we're just trying to bring [these values] back."[22]

What permeates many businesses flush with customer evangelists: employee evangelists. The tone inside company headquarters in St. Louis is meant to reflect the values that Clark espouses. One could say it's downright dot-com. Dogs and kids are welcome amid the colorful hallways and desks. There's flexible scheduling, telecommuting, and 15 "honey days" of vacation a year. All bathrooms are equipped with diaper-changing stations. There's a playroom for kids. Titles are decidedly unstuffy. Clark is CEB: chief executive bear. Most business cards include the word *bear* in the title.

Each employee spends three weeks in St. Louis at Bear University. Classes impart "the Way of the Bear," a distillation of the company's culture, its values, and its expectations for customer service. The company's chief marketing bear says there's a perfectly good reason to devote three weeks of training for every employee.

"It's about building relationships," Chief Marketing Bear Kroll says. "It goes between the relationships of our business partners, our guests, and our associates. In building those relationships, people walk away with smiles, feel good, feel rewarded, and feel all of the things you and I want to feel every day."[23]

Clark says store managers have usually worked at other successful children's retail companies, themed entertainment parks, or restaurants. The experience of their master bear builders is more varied, "but a love of kids and an outgoing personality are musts!" In 2001, a magazine named Build-A-Bear Workshop the number one "Best Place to Work."[24]

Connecting with causes is another big part of the company's strategy. Its list of charitable causes is extensive and a reflection of Clark's concerns. There's the company's partnership with the World Wildlife Fund (WWF), whose mission is to protect wildlife and wildlands. Build-A-Bear Workshop created a Bengal tiger and a giant panda whose sales benefit the World Wildlife Fund. After three years, the company has sold 150,000 animals that have benefited the WWF.

There's also the company's partnership with the Humane Society. One dollar is donated to the society for each black Labrador toy sold. A popular program with shoppers, the company sold 100,000 black Lab toys in the first six months of the program.

In 2001, during breast cancer awareness month, the company partnered with the Susan G. Komen Breast Cancer Foundation and the Siteman Cancer Center to unveil a Hopeful Wishes bear. Sales of the bear benefit breast cancer research, treatment, and support.

In May 2001, the company launched a "Stuffed with Hugs" day. It encourages children to participate in social causes by inviting them into the company's stores to create a teddy bear that's donated to the Teddy Bear Foundation, a nonprofit organization that helps children in crisis. Kroll

says 15,000 teddy bears created by children went to kids who live in shelters as a result of neglect or abuse.

The company created teachme.buildabear.com in partnership with Scholastic, Inc. Multimedia flash cards quiz kids on math and geography using all of the Build-A-Bear Workshop iconography, type usage, and color palettes. A separate section helps educators with lesson plans on "friendship and cultural awareness."

"I think the cause-related positioning we have taken shows that this company cares so much about its guests, its business partners, and social issues; and it's something that other companies should assess," Kroll says. "Where do you get the best benefit: Is it on price or on building a relationship? Build-A-Bear Workshop is all about building relationships."[25]

Lessons learned:

- Connect with causes that reflect the company's values.
- Create an atmosphere for employees and customers to feel they are joining a club.

ACHIEVING FAST AND RESPONSIVE EVENT-DRIVEN MARKETING

During a drive one night in February 2002 on the way to her home in St. Louis, Clark was deconstructing what was wrong with retailing today. She took precise aim at a national department store that had announced it no longer accepts returns 30 days after purchase. As a result, "I don't shop there anymore," she says. "That changed my attitude about the store. They are saying, 'we don't value your business; you are not important to us . . . and I've spent thousands of dollars a year there."

Build-A-Bear Workshop's return policy: No time limits. Full refunds. Responsive. If customers need to use the phone, no problem. "And you can be sure the bathrooms are clean, too," Clark says.[26]

Part of the company's strategy is to keep a relatively small inventory of product items, which usually hovers near 300. A limited inventory keeps costs down and product fresh. How does the company handle inventory that isn't selling? "We stop buying it!" Clark says emphatically. "We have very accurate testing procedures, and this rarely happens—so far."[27] If a retailer is not driven by low prices or markdowns, it must then be driven by originality and newness, Clark contends. That's what drives customers.

Part of Build-A-Bear Workshop's marketing strategy is "event craziness." There are special St. Patrick's Day and Valentine's Day bears; a "spring furry fashion show" with spring clothes; a teddy bear centennial carnival. (Teddy Roosevelt's birthday is a company holiday. The teddy bear is named after the former U.S. president, who is said to have spared the life of a bear cub during a hunting trip in 1902.) Throughout 2002, the company commemorated the 100-year anniversary of the teddy bear's creation. It's a department store for creatures of the woods.

Birthdays are a big part of the company's event marketing strategy. Because Build-A-Bear Workshop knows the birthdays of its customers (and the "birthday" of every animal created), it sends reminder notices to the parents of children 90 days in advance, "telling them it's time to plan a party," Clark says, adding that this type of tactic is turning the company into something of a direct marketer.

"We know the birthday of the people who have bought a gift and the persons to whom they are sending the gift," she says. "But mostly, people make things for themselves."[28]

The company advertises in specialty magazines, but its influence is understated, Kroll says. "Wal-Mart and Target and all those other guys have their Sunday supplements, and they spend beaucoup dollars on them," Kroll adds. "It's predictable and everyone expects it. With us, it's just not that way."[29]

The company's weekly customer surveys ask customers how they first heard about the store. According to Clark, nearly half of the customers answer it was from a customer evangelist. Adding to evidence that retail is still about "location, location, location," 40 percent of customers say they stumbled across it in a mall. The remaining 10 percent heard about the store through the media or advertising.

For Kroll, whose marketing budget includes public relations, the company's Web site, and advertising, word of mouth is her most effective tool, one that largely takes care of itself.

"This has been the most overwhelming and luxury situation that I have found myself in," she says, laughing.[30]

Data supplied by comScore Networks, which measures online usage patterns, show the average visitor spends about 16 minutes on the Build-A-Bear Workshop Web site, viewing about 17 pages. At the end of 2001, when these measurements were taken, about 137,000 people visited the site each month.

"They leave our stores in a euphoric stage, and they go home and they get online," Kroll says.[31]

After the events of September 11, 2001, Build-A-Bear Workshop responded by sending thousands of teddy bears to children who had lost a parent or relative in the attacks. It was Kroll's second day. She had just moved to St. Louis from New York City.

"All we did was sit in the cafeteria with the TV on, trying to think of what we could do to help," Kroll says. "The next day, we had thousands upon thousands of stuffed animals going to children with families who had suspected, or in fact knew, that they had lost a loved one. We were getting calls from the Northeast on a minute-by-minute basis asking us to please send something to comfort these children. We would just do whatever it took. There were no parameters."[32]

The company encouraged kids to visit its stores and help create the emergency bears. About 11,000 in total were sent.

To respond to frequent customer questions about the proper care techniques for their toys, the company launched an annual "Bear Care Training" program in 1998. Promoted only to existing customers, the program is a popular annual checkup for the Build-A-Bear Workshop toys (including those purchased somewhere else) to fix loose and broken stitching or fluff up the stuffing.

"People start calling us in January asking when it is," Clark says. "It's a big weekend."

By providing free mending services, the store also makes it easy for customers to update their bear's wardrobe or buy additional animals.

"It always exceeds our expectations [of] what people purchase" during the program, Clark says.[33]

Build-A-Bear Workshop has taken the idea of mass customization and made it a responsive, adaptable marketing strategy across a 100-store enterprise. For instance, customers said they wanted to dress their bears in the apparel of their alma maters. Now, each store features accessories of its nearby colleges and universities. Each store's home city is well represented by products as well.

It's as if Maxine Clark is a kid again, shopping with her mother at Burdines in downtown Miami and enjoying the rooftop circus.

Lessons learned:

- Keep your products new.
- Be relevant in the world of events that are important to your customers.
- Develop flexible company policies that are in tune with customer priorities.

EVANGELISM SCORECARD: BUILD-A-BEAR WORKSHOP

Customer Plus-Delta

- The company continually solicits customer feedback, aligning it with compensation.

- Ninety-nine percent of the company's ideas for new products have come from customers.
- The company loves e-mail and encourages customers to send ideas, suggestions, and complaints—about 6,000 emails arrive each month.

Napsterized Knowledge

- The company was founded on the idea that manufacturing is fun and should be part of the customer process.
- The company's Bear University employee training program is three weeks long.
- All customer feedback is shared throughout the company.

Build the Buzz

- A unique and personalized bear creation process creates buzz and word of mouth.
- A Cub Condo replaces the traditional shopping bag that customers carry around the mall.
- An extensive Web site is filled with dozens of opportunities to tell a friend.

Create Community

- Extensive relationships exist with nonprofits that support breast cancer research and treatment, the World Wildlife Fund, and the American Humane Society.
- The company makes direct appeals to collector communities with limited edition products.

Bite-Size Chunks

- Stores host parties and events for kids, some of whom are introduced to the store for the first time.
- The company offers its products through select third parties and channels, such as FTD.
- An expansive Web site, Buildabear.com, tries to re-create an in-store experience.

Create a Cause

- Clark launched the company with the objective of changing the American retail experience.
- The company's extensive involvement with charitable organizations tells customers it stands for a number of causes; the efforts also produce extensive favorable publicity.

Coordinates

Company:	Build-A-Bear Workshop, Inc.
Headquarters:	St. Louis, Missouri
Founded:	1997
Chief executive:	Maxine Clark
Marketing chief:	Teresa Kroll
Description:	"An interactive retail experience"
Industry:	Retail
Employees:	2,400
Ownership:	Privately held
Web site:	<www.buildabear.com>
Number of stores:	70 at this writing, with 100 by the end of 2002

CHAPTER | 14

A CAUSE, NOT JUST AN AIRLINE
southwest airlines

"Why the hell should I spend money on focus groups? I read
every letter customers write." [1]

—COLLEEN BARRETT, president and COO of Southwest Airlines

Southwest Airlines receives about 3,900 customer letters every month. Some complain about delayed flights, lost baggage, and other systemic ills associated with air travel.

But the company estimates that at least three-fourths of all the correspondents thank the company for good service, commending a flight attendant or requesting that Southwest establish service in a new city.

Then terrorists hijacked four passenger jets on September 11, 2001, crashing two of them into the World Trade Center in New York, one into the Pentagon in Washington, D.C., and another in a Pennsylvania field. Estimates are that 3,054 people were killed. Even though none of Southwest's planes were involved in the attacks and none of its employees were lost in the debris of destroyed buildings and lives, the company was significantly affected nonetheless.

Among the hundreds of new challenges the United States and the world suddenly faced, one was key to Dallas-based Southwest: Would the American aviation industry recover?

Air travel is the engine of hundreds, perhaps thousands, of local economies. As such, a crippled airline industry poses huge risks for the economies of the United States and other countries. After the attacks on 9/11, American airspace was completely shut down for 48 hours. It took more than a week for airlines to gather their bearings after resuming flights.

Worse yet, palpable fear gripped the United States, especially for air travelers. Airline passenger counts dropped dramatically.

The letters to Southwest's headquarters started changing. Customers wrote letters filled with emotion, expressing sorrow for what had happened. They worried that Southwest's famous cash reserves—over $1 billion—were being quickly depleted by flying nearly empty planes.

Remarkably, many of the letters included money. There were checks for $5, $10, even $500. Many returned travel vouchers or gift certificates.

"After the initial shock of the attack subsided, I began to worry about the smiling people that work for Southwest," one writer wrote in a letter the company provided for review. "Having said that, I want to return this $100 in SWA gift certificates that one of your customer service agents sent me after I informed him of my first and only bad experience with Southwest Airlines. I wish I could send you more than $100, but this is all I have."[2]

The company's employees were the biggest givers. They requested a fund be set up for those who wanted to pledge portions of their salary to keep the airline afloat and profitable. Total employee contributions were $1.3 million for what employees called the LUV fund.

The goodwill Southwest had cultivated outside and inside the company since its launch in 1973 was paying off.

"We have customers who have rallied to the cause of Southwest Airlines," says CEO Jim Parker.[3]

Southwest Airlines creates customer evangelists because:

- Freedom is its rallying cause.
- Customer evangelism begins with employee evangelism.
- The company loves customer input.
- The best customers are treated like the royalty they are.
- It enmeshes itself with communities.

FREEDOM AS ITS RALLYING CAUSE

The spirit of Southwest is an embodiment of the freewheeling personality of the company's co-founder and chairman, Herb Kelleher—a rabble-rouser and maverick. He rides a Harley to work, chain smokes furiously, and professes an undying love for Wild Turkey whiskey. He's a cut-up who, it could be safely argued, is a free spirit.

Trained as a lawyer, Kelleher once challenged another company's CEO to arm wrestle their dispute over using the "just plane smart" catchphrase. The resulting spectacle—so completely over the top that the World Wrestling Federation's Vince McMahon would have blushed—was a public relations bonanza.

Halloween is a sacred day at the company, thanks to Kelleher's love of costumes. He has publicly donned outfits portraying himself as a wrestler, Elvis, and as a band major. The company's early uniforms for flight attendants featured hot pants. Now, it's only the mannequins in company headquarters who wear the company's early Barbarellalike outfits; flight attendants in 2002 wore more conventional long pants or shorts.

Thirty-three years after its launch, Dallas-based Southwest Airlines is a responsive army of 33,000 passionate employees. It is often number one or two on *Fortune* magazine's list of the best American employers. It does $5.7 billion per year in business and has outlasted competitors big and small to build a $14 billion company valuation that's bigger than competitors United, American, and Continental combined. It has been profitable every quarter and every year since 1973.

Although revenues dropped significantly in the financial quarter after the September 11, 2001, attacks, it still earned a profit of $151 million. American, Delta, United, and others furloughed 115,000 workers and lost a combined $4 billion. Southwest kept all of its employees after September 11 and paid the wages lost to its skycaps, who largely work for tips.

"We have a duty to protect the jobs of our people," Parker says of the company's decision to not join other carriers with massive layoffs.

After a remarkable 35-year run as an airline industry pioneer, Kelleher relinquished his presidency and CEO titles in June 2001, making Parker CEO and then chief people officer Colleen Barrett president.

"When we were deciding how to divide up Herb's responsibilities, we decided that Colleen would take all of the smoking, and I would handle all of the drinking," Parker says in his deadpan Texas drawl.[4]

Barrett started her career as Kelleher's secretary and rose through the ranks in part by sending birthday cards to employees, personally responding to customer letters, and being a tireless company champion. She is credited for shaping and maintaining the company's culture. Her analysis for the company's success: "Southwest is a cause, not a career."[5]

The company's competitive strategy, listed below, is free of complexity.

- Fly Boeing 737s only—it simplifies the operational skills needed for mechanics and pilots.
- Fly direct routes only and avoid the common hub-and-spoke passenger system, thereby making the company less susceptible to delays.

- Do not pay millions of dollars to be part of other airlines' computer reservation systems.

The evidence for the clarity of this strategy abounds. In the first half of 2001, while other airlines struggled with huge losses, strike threats, and growing concern over customer dissatisfaction, Southwest remained profitable, accident free, and hovering near the top of government-issued performance metrics. Since its maiden flight in 1971, Southwest has had only one work strike.

The company has grown almost completely organically. It has avoided owning car rental agencies and reservation systems, strategies favored by competitors like UAL Corporation, parent of United Airlines, and AMR, parent of American Airlines. In late 2001, UAL CEO James Goodwin wrote in an e-mail to company employees that the company was "hemorrhaging money," which "has to be stopped—and soon—or United will perish sometime next year."[6]

The flight attendants of Southwest Airlines are well known for a wacky sense of humor, which generates tremendous buzz; an Internet search, in fact, for "Southwest flight attendants" and "humor" yields almost 1,000 Web pages. Customers obviously love capturing the humor of Southwest and sharing it. The flight attendants have been quoted as saying:

- "Here at Southwest, we flight attendants get up real early and go to the airport so we can sign up for a flight with the most handsome pilots. When you are departing the aircraft, look in the cockpit and you'll see that today we slept late."
- "There may be 50 ways to leave your lover, but there are only 4 ways out of this airplane."
- "We will be serving meat loaf today, which you can use as a flotation device."
- "The captain will be turning down the lights as we prepare for takeoff. This isn't necessary for any technical purpose. It's just been a long day and our flight attendants don't look as lovely as they did this morning."[7]

Southwest has also freed itself from serving meals on its flights, thereby avoiding the costs associated with something that customers hate anyway.

In the fiercely competitive airline industry, it's easy to go from pioneer to chump. Some pioneers were respected for their smarts but disliked for their abrasive personalities, such as American Airlines' longtime leader Robert Crandall. Many pioneer airlines have disappeared altogether: TWA, Eastern, and Braniff are several of the better known ones to have checked out. Southwest launched its business in 1967, only to fight a four-year legal battle to get its first plane off the ground.

By consistently focusing on low costs and high customer satisfaction, Southwest has led all other competitors in metrics the FAA uses to measure airline performance: flight delays, mishandled baggage, oversales, and consumer complaints.

"I was talking at the Yale Graduate School of Business some years ago," Kelleher once told an interviewer. "In the Q&A session, one of the students stood up and said, 'It seems to me you're talking more about a religion than a business.' And I said, 'If you feel that way about your business, I think that's good. That's a plus.'"[8]

Lessons learned:

- Employees and customers understand clearly what the company stands for.
- Southwest's maverick culture helps it avoid the convention and duplicity that would result from following the lead of others.
- Its company strategy follows its cause, not the other way around.

EMPLOYEE EVANGELISM: THE ORIGIN OF CUSTOMER EVANGELISM

What Southwest's customers experience begins behind the scenes. A Southwest "all-hands" meeting provides some evidence of a company that is close-knit, gregarious, and huggy.

On a chilly night in March 2002, about 700 Southwest employees from a dozen different cities gathered in a Chicago high school near Midway Airport—directly under the flight path of departing Southwest jets—to hear CEO Jim Parker and President Colleen Barrett provide a "state of the company" update. Before the event began, everyone happily hugged one another and even strangers. Thousands of hugs were distributed and almost as many kisses—most on the cheek, others on the lips—were given and received like candy at a parade. Barrett is a prodigious hugger; on this night, with her two-foot-long gray ponytail, gray knit pants, gray Southwest Airlines T-shirt, and bright red sneakers, employees lined up for her hugs.

CEO Jim Parker is all Texan: he's tall and big. In his jeans, denim shirt, and unmistakable Texas accent delivered in measured deadpan, Parker seems to be an all-business cattle rancher. But he's a lawyer, trained at the University of Texas, and had been Southwest's general counsel since 1986. When the meeting began and Parker introduced, the crowd leaped to its feet for a minute-long ovation. After September 11, the company and the industry had endured challenges unprecedented since the dawn of commercial aviation; the audience was obviously grateful to Parker for Southwest's avoiding layoffs and remaining profitable.

He and Barrett had a secondary challenge to overcome on this night and in the years ahead: being the company's leaders after Kelleher's retirement. Parker endeared himself by telling a long and funny lawyer joke (as many lawyer jokes often do, this one culminated in the simultaneous destruction of hundreds of lawyers at once, making clear that Parker doesn't take himself too seriously).

His "state of the company" report was to the point. The company had, to date, weathered the most significant crisis in its history. With detectable emotion, he discussed the company's "duty to employees to protect jobs" and reported no one was laid off after the September attacks. When he announced that 11 percent of the company's profits had been added to the employee profit-sharing plan, the crowd erupted into cheers.

Nonetheless, Parker said, passenger load levels were still down. The company would be hard-pressed to deliver a profitable first quarter. (The company later announced an 82 percent drop in year-over-year income but managed to post a profit.) The company's situation remains serious, he said, and cost cutting was still a top priority.

Barrett was introduced next, also to an extended standing ovation. Onstage, Barrett is a laconic cutup, part Southern sass, part Roseanne. Like her longtime mentor and boss, Herb Kelleher, Barrett says what's on her mind, the antithesis of a stereotypical Fortune 500 executive. She even enjoys whining a bit, which appears to be part of her charm.

Barrett is often credited with being the glue in the company's culture. A 24-year company veteran who started as Kelleher's secretary to eventually become president, Barrett's maverick nature is a natural continuation of Kelleher's legacy. Barrett's approach is to read every customer letter and often respond to them herself.

At a question-and-answer session with employees, someone asked the duo about the monetary contributions that customers made after September 11.

"I wanted to give it all back, but Jim wanted to keep it," Barrett quipped.[9] Company spokesperson Linda Rutherford said the company didn't keep an exact tally, but the total was "hundreds and hundreds" of dollars.[10]

Kevin Krone, vice president for interactive marketing at Southwest, explains the company's employee evangelism this way: "I think a lot of companies miss that you have to take care of your employees. They're not an expense item on an income statement; you can't look at it that way. They are one of your biggest assets. They can literally make or break you. Taking care of them is as important as taking care of your paying customers."[11]

Prospective employees are asked how humor helped them out of a difficult situation. Pilot candidates are sometimes asked to don Southwest shorts; the ones who see the request as fun can make it to the next round of interviews. Those who see it as beneath them end up working somewhere else.

The culture inside Southwest Airlines is devoted to freedom, which the company has transferred to its marketing: the freedom to be an individual (highly encouraged) and to have a sense of humor (encouraged more).

"In our hearts, we know that we have the best employees in the world," Parker says. "The Golden Rule is pretty important here."[12]

Company headquarters features thousands upon thousands of pictures of employees on the walls of its two-story headquarters. Southwest President Colleen Barrett despises empty walls, so nearly every square foot of company walls features framed pictures of employees in action at work, pictures of their kids and families, pictures in their high school cheerleading uniforms. Like a proud mama, the company even frames its employees' artwork and hangs it on the wall.

Colleen Barrett chairs a committee of employees from every area of the company. Known as the Culture Committee, its purpose is to build on the company's effervescent personality throughout the employee ranks. The results allow Southwest to retain a familylike atmosphere amidst rapid growth.

"People who emphasize too strongly the fact that they're professionals usually are not very good at what they do," Kelleher says. "What really adds up to professionalism is being very good at what you do in a very modest way."[13]

Lessons learned:

- Hire employees who believe in your company's cause.
- A fun workplace translates into a fun environment for customers.
- Take explicit measures to preserve the company culture.

LOVING CUSTOMER INPUT

Kelleher is well known for flying on Southwest's planes to talk with customers and employees. One frequent flyer in Texas has sat next to Kelleher three times in ten years. Each time, Kelleher asked him and others nearby how well Southwest was doing in a number of areas, looking for trends, spotting inconsistencies.

This strategy comes from a customer-focused belief. "We tell our people, 'Don't worry about profit. Think about customer service.' Profit is a by-product of customer service. It's not an end in and of itself," Kelleher says.[14]

Back-office managers are encouraged to spend a day doing frontline jobs, such as working the gate or ticket counter, to hear customer issues firsthand and help solve recurring problems.

In an article he penned for the Peter F. Drucker Foundation in 1997, Kelleher described the company's marketing strategy: "We market ourselves based on the personality and spirit of ourselves. That sounds like an easy claim, but, in fact, it is a supremely dangerous position to stake out because if you're wrong, customers will let you know—with a vengeance. Customers are like a force of nature: You can't fool them, and you ignore them at your own peril."[15]

Even though the company has created customer evangelists partly because of its emphasis on creating a dialogue with them, it does not accept e-mail. A page on the company's Web site explains:

> Call us traditional, but we elect to steer clear of the chat-style, respond-on-demand, quick casual format and focus on meaningful Customer dialogue. This is not because we don't care. It's because that style counters our 30 plus year commitment to Customer Service.
>
> Our Customers deserve accurate, specific, personal, and professionally written answers, and it takes time to research, investigate, and compose a real business letter. We answer every letter we receive in the order it arrives, and we streamline in order to keep our costs low, our People productive, our operating efficiency high, and our responses warm and personal.[16]

Arriving in that mailbag each month are requests from cities that the airline establish service in their airports. There were 165 requests in 2001, but Southwest prides itself on slow, continuous growth and a culture of maintaining low expectations. Because the company encourages and receives so much customer feedback, the prevailing attitude toward focus groups is pretty clear. "Why the hell should I spend money on focus groups?" Barrett asks. "I read every letter customers write."[17]

The company avoids most traditional forms of long-range planning and instead favors an integrated, customer-focused plan that incorporates societal trends and how Southwest intends to fit within that trend. Many people outside Southwest's executive circle are involved in this process.

Lessons learned:

- Company leaders can get direct input from customers by going where the customers are.
- Respond to all customer input with a personalized response.

TREATING YOUR BEST CUSTOMERS LIKE THE ROYALTY THEY ARE

Rich Marcotte is the mayor of Southwest Airlines.

For nine years, he was Southwest's most frequent flyer out of Chicago, traveling at least 200 times a year while he was national marketing director for USA Tax Help in the 1990s.

His typical schedule was to board a flight on a Sunday and fly to one of 20 client cities; return Tuesday night; fly again on Wednesday night to another client city; return Friday. Until 2001, he did this every week for nine years.

Along the way, Marcotte was nicknamed the "Mayor of Southwest" by the wife of a frequent-flyer rival. She joked about Marcotte's mayorlike persona in Southwest's gate areas. Although he doesn't fly as much for his new job, Marcotte still works each gate like a local politico, shaking hands, talking up business, professing a love for "his" airline, and pulling angry or frustrated travelers aside and calming them down. He signs up fellow passengers for Rapid Rewards, the company's frequent-flier program. Marcotte is a volunteer ambassador and salesperson for a company he describes as "family."

"It was a crazy schedule I had, but I enjoyed it because of Southwest," Marcotte says. "It's easy to tell friends and associates about something when you feel passionate about it. I've never seen an organization like it.

"I was treated like royalty."[18]

Because he was the company's best customer in the Midwest and because he got along with Southwest's Chicago team so well, the company treated him well outside the terminal. They gave him tickets to the NBA finals when Michael Jordan was the king of Chicago. They gave him the opportunity to throw out the first pitch at a Chicago Cubs game, as shown in Figure 14.1.

Southwest's regional marketing director, Patty Kryscha, ensured that Marcotte had a chance to meet his hero, Herb Kelleher.

Marcotte estimates that at 200 trips per year for nine years and evangelizing Southwest to several people per trip, he's probably directly influenced at least 9,000 customers for the company. He's even volunteered to go out on the speaking circuit and address audiences on behalf of the airline if he was needed.

Says CEO Parker of the company's customer evangelists: "The reason we have loyal customers is they've been touched by a Southwest Airlines employee."[19]

Lessons learned:

- Pay special attention to your best customer evangelists.

Figure 14.1 | Flyer Marcotte Throwing a Strike at a Chicago Cubs Game

Rich Marcotte throws a strike at a Chicago Cubs game at Wrigley Field. Arranged for his behalf by Southwest's regional marketing director, throwing out the first pitch of a game was one of the many benefits Marcotte enjoyed by being one of Southwest's best customers and most prolific evangelists.

ENMESHING WITH COMMUNITIES

Patty Kryscha doesn't have a long white beard, red suit, or reindeer sleigh. But she could be easily mistaken for the female version of Kris Kringle; she even has a jolly laugh.

A 22-year Southwest veteran, Kryscha is regional director of the company's Chicago field marketing office. Her job is to be the company's ambassador and develop relationships with the communities in Chicago, Indianapolis, Nashville, and Columbus by doling out gifts on behalf of Southwest Airlines. With her trove of plane tickets, gift certificates, and a modest marketing budget, Kryscha and her six-person team sort through 550 requests every year from local organizations, deciding who's naughty and who's nice.

In 2001, the Chicago field office donated 136 tickets to the local chapter of 67 different organizations, such as Big Brothers/Big Sisters, the YMCA, and the American Diabetes Association. Kryscha's office also donated 280 gift certificates ranging from $25 to $400 to groups such as the San Miguel School, the Blue Island Police Department, and the Mount Greenwood Little League.

United and American Airlines tend to sponsor symphonies and arts events, whereas Southwest typically supports good ol'-fashioned professional sports. Southwest has been involved with the Chicago Cubs since the company started service there in 1985. Kryscha says the partnership makes perfect sense because "Southwest is fun and the Cubs are fun."[20]

The company's most frequent flyers are often invited to party with Kryscha and her crew at Wrigley Field, sometimes offering customers besides Rich Marcotte the chance to throw out the first pitch at games. "People here are passionate about the Cubs," Kryscha says, "so there is some transference."

But don't think that playing the role of Kringle is easy. "We get requests from so many deserving nonprofit organizations [for tickets or sponsorships]," Kryscha says. "The challenge is trying to decide who needs our help the most."[21]

But that doesn't stop some of the "bleacher bums" from getting creative with their requests, like the group of fraternity brothers who called to ask Kryscha to comp the group's annual beer blast to New Orleans for Mardi Gras. It was for a good cause, they said, and they might raise a little bit of money, too. That got the naughty stamp.

Kryscha and her team donate more than company freebies. Many times after work or during weekends they are volunteering for many of the local causes they believe in. They also consult with nonprofits on employee relations, serve on the boards of social services agencies, and mentor children through the YMCA. "Southwest encourages us to get involved," she says. "It's nice to have the freedom and flexibility to do that."[22]

Lessons learned:

- Supporting local causes with products and services shows your company cares.
- Give employees the flexibility to work with local nonprofits and showcase their skills and talents.

EVANGELISM SCORECARD: SOUTHWEST AIRLINES

Customer Plus-Delta

- Kelleher sets the tone for executives to fly as passengers to get firsthand customer feedback.
- The company encourages customers to write and acknowledges every note with a handwritten response.
- Back-office managers are encouraged to work frontline jobs to hear directly from customers.

Build the Buzz

- Quirky and fun flight attendants get customers talking.
- Employees are encouraged to show their personality.
- Pay attention to detail; always call people back and bestow smiles.

Create Community

- Local field offices develop personal relationships with top local customers.
- Local field offices get involved in supporting community causes.
- Southwest supports employees' personal involvement in community causes.

Bite-Size Chunks

- Southwest initiated a "Friends Fly Free" promotion.
- It has holiday sales to encourage people to fly.

Create a Cause

- Southwest's cause is freedom—company strategy follows its cause, not the other way around.
- Employees and customers understand what the company stands for.

Coordinates

Company:	Southwest Airlines
Headquarters:	Dallas, Texas
Founded:	1967
CEO:	Jim Parker
Marketing chief:	Joyce Rogge
Description:	Airline
Industry:	Travel
Employees:	33,000
Ownership:	Publicly traded (NYSE: LUV)
Web site:	<www.southwest.com>

CHAPTER 15

THE BILLION-DOLLAR CAUSE
IBM

*"To be honest, we'd open source just about anything the
[Linux] community wanted."* [1]

—IRVING WLADAWSKY-BERGER, vice president of technology strategy, IBM

A wave called Linux is heading toward the shoreline of computer operating system supremacy, and IBM is doing its best to ride it.

This isn't your father's IBM.

Big Blue has committed $1 billion to ride the Linux wave. Linux is the
free computer operating system that isn't controlled by Microsoft, Apple,
or any other computer company. The life of Linux is determined by a
"gated community" of programmers who, while working at varying companies, also donate their time to developing the operating system; they collaborate on writing the software so that it will run any computer.
Companies like IBM package Linux on their various computers with ac-
companying software.

Linux began as a project in 1991 for creator Linus Torvalds to learn
more about the Intel 386 processor. Torvalds was a student at the University
of Helsinki in Finland, and a posting to a computer bulletin board in
August of that year announced his intentions.

I'm doing a (free) operating system (just a hobby, won't be big
and professional like gnu) for 386 (486) AT clones. This has been
brewing since April, and is starting to get ready. I'd like any feed-

back on things people like/dislike in minix, as my OS resembles it somewhat (same physical layout of the file-system (due to practical reasons among other things).[2]

Torvalds's post caught the attention of other programmers, and within a few years he had a small army of volunteers providing feedback and writing components of what he eventually called Linux, a play on the Unix operating system.

The growth of Linux has been a grassroots phenomenon. Because Linux doesn't present expensive licensing issues like proprietary computer operating systems and the software continues to grow and evolve based on the needs of its users, it was inevitable that Linux would become as popular as it has. That IBM has invested $1 billion into making Linux part of its core strategy has added another level of legitimacy to Linux and the notion of open source software.

With its big billion bucks, IBM is investing in Linux development centers around the world, training sales, marketing, and professional services experts to evangelize Linux to customers and developers. It is giving away $40 million worth of Linux software tools to encourage open source software developers to create Linux applications. About 2,000 IBM programmers are developing Linux versions of the company's entire suite of software products. But when it comes to Linux, the open source community sets the rules and agenda, not IBM.

IBM has configured its entire vast line of servers—the computers that store and serve files, programs, and data—to run Linux. These include everything from the company's $1,500 Internet servers to its $3 million mainframes. Like most revolutions in history, one man is leading the charge that is occurring inside the largest technology company in the world.

Meet Irving Wladawsky-Berger, IBM evangelist.

Wait just a nanosecond here. IBM? Evangelism?

The Cuban-born Wladawsky-Berger, who has a Ph.D. in physics, is the unstoppable force behind IBM's bold bet. His Linux strategy may eventually make the company less Dickensian and more Silicon Valley. He is a lifelong IBMer who began his career in IBM's research labs. Wladawksy-Berger has consistently been on the leading edge of the company's technology efforts. In the 1980s, he was responsible for IBM's supercomputer efforts; in the mid-1990s, he was tasked with bringing the company into the age of the Internet.

The idea of IBM's creating customer evangelists seems a stretch, though, especially for a company known for its bureaucracy. That IBM was declared a monopolist by the federal government in 1969 has also been a nearly insurmountable challenge to creating customer evangelists.

IBM of the 1970s was like Microsoft of the 1990s: It exerted vast amounts of control, power, and influence but lacked an extensive network of customer evangelists. The old saying that "no one was ever fired for hiring IBM" was true because few alternatives existed.

But in 2002, this was a story of evangelism in the making. IBM's embrace of an open source computer operating system is remarkable. Linux is the embodiment of what a community of like-minded and passionate individuals can achieve when they band together.

Among the community of several hundred thousand developers IBM is courting, there is cautious, but growing, support. IBM has the makings for creating customer evangelists. It is on the road to creating evangelists because:

- It's embracing a cause as much as a technology.
- The company is lending support and credibility to a community.
- IBM is making large portions of its intellectual property widely available.

EMBRACING A CAUSE AS MUCH AS A TECHNOLOGY

In announcing the company's $1 billion investment during the eBusiness Conference and Expo in 2000, then IBM chief executive Lou Gerstner said IBM "is convinced that Linux can do for business applications what the Internet did for networking and communications."[3]

By following the open standards and collaboration that fueled the development and rapid growth of the Internet, IBM is hoping it can do the same with Linux and open source software. But what is open source software, anyway? Eric S. Raymond documents its brief but influential history in the book *The Cathedral & the Bazaar*. He writes that Linux was the first project "for which a conscious and successful effort to use the entire *world* as its talent pool was made."[4] (Raymond's emphasis.)

Open source software is akin to a local barn raising or a Habitat for Humanity home-building project: Like-minded people who may or may not know one another organize under a common goal to build something that will benefit a group of individuals and the community at large. The source of the software—the code that powers it—is open and available for anyone in the community to examine. By its nature, open source software is typically free or very inexpensive. It's that global talent pool and its key influencers whom IBM is courting. Some are responsible for purchasing hardware and software, whereas others recommend what to buy.

In 2002, IBM was evangelizing a future of Linuxcentric computing, and for good reason. International Data Corporation (IDC) predicted that Linux will command 38 percent of the server market by 2004, making it the most popular operating system in the world.

How big, then, is the community that IBM is courting?

"No one has done census work on this," says Jeff "Hemos" Bates, the executive editor of online technology community slashdot.org. He says that estimates are somewhere in the hundreds of thousands. "Welcome to the glory of counting."[5]

How are some of the leaders of the open source community reacting to IBM's efforts? In April 2002, it is mostly with support, tempered with some skepticism. "IBM has done far more and made a greater investment in Linux than any other major vendor," concludes IDC analyst Dan Kusnetzky.[6]

Microsoft controls the majority of operating systems with its own software, which it spends hundreds of millions of dollars developing, and earns even more from selling it. Linux, which lies at the heart of what's known as the open source software movement, makes Microsoft very nervous.

Twenty years ago, before Microsoft was more than just a DOS blip on the radar screen, the idea that any computer anywhere being controlled by anything other than IBM software would have been such an unfathomable idea that you may have just as well pictured Ross Perot as a dope-smoking hippie.

IBM launched its Linux strategy with a brilliant iconic campaign. (See Figure 15.1.) The three symbols representing peace, love, and a penguin were instantly recognizable. (The penguin is the symbol that represents Linux; the familiar cartoon logo of the Linux penguin was designed by Larry Ewing. Linux creator Torvalds settled on the penguin icon because the flightless birds are usually considered "cute, cuddly, and contented" but can also charge at an unwary visitor at what seems to be "100 mph.")

To give its cause for Linux street credibility with the skeptical programmer crowd, IBM went to the streets, literally. In Chicago and San Francisco, IBM's ad agency was supposed to have stenciled the three icons at busy intersections using biodegradable chalk. But somehow the agency ended up using a fairly permanent spray paint. IBM claimed ignorance of the effort and paid fines to clean up the graffiti, but the publicity surrounding the stunts proved to be invaluable and helped show that Big Blue "ain't" so stodgy anymore.

An IBM television commercial announced the launch. "They stole all our servers!" a clueless operations manager announces to the police, but a savvy techie casually mentions they were merely consolidated onto one IBM mainframe running Linux. After the launch, there was little ambiguity that IBM stood behind Linux in a new and offbeat way.

Figure 15.1 | **IBM's Campaign to Launch Linux Support**

IBM's marketing campaign to launch its Linux initiative highlighted Peace/Love/ Penguin logos that were spray painted on city sidewalks around the country. Although some municipalities were not amused by the stunt and subsequently fined IBM and its marketing agency, the campaign garnered plenty of publicity and probably helped the company's overall "street credibility."[7]

"We are members of an industry that's out to change the world," Wladawsky-Berger told *Linux Magazine.*

LENDING SUPPORT AND CREDIBILITY TO A COMMUNITY

At the 2001 LinuxWorld Conference and Expo, then IBM president Sam Palmisano (later promoted to chief executive officer) underscored the company's courting of the Linux community in the hope of making it evangelists.

"Change—some are excited about it, some really threatened about it," he said, making not-so-sly references to Microsoft and Sun, which have held very public contempt for Linux. "You are the community that will get this done. But we need to work together."[8]

That encouragement means constant courting of a community loosely organized around belief in the ideals of a cooperative. As explained by Tim O'Reilly, founder and president of O'Reilly & Associates and widely considered one of the leaders of the open source community: "Open Source is really a gift culture in which you gain status by what you give away."[9]

Even though IBM is making inroads, hurdles remain. It rankled some to hear IBM's Linux evangelist Wladawsky-Berger say: "The more we encourage the development of Linux, the more it will drive our business."[10]

"The comments that IBM has made that their support for Linux is predicated on not just a belief in open source, but that it will help their business, to my mind means they are not changing their DNA," says slashdot.org's Bates, whose skepticism for IBM's motives are representative of many in the technology community. "They are finding that they can be a better business by supporting Linux, and that's not changing your DNA—that's being a smarter business, and I think IBM deserves support for that."[11]

But O'Reilly insists that IBM has so far made the right moves.

"I thought IBM did a great job out of the gate," O'Reilly said. "They quickly organized a tiger team to look into it, flew a bunch of outsiders in to brief their team, and formulated a policy. There are always skeptics, but in general I'd say that IBM has done a better job than most of the big companies at getting the open source community on its side. It's made real contributions to a number of projects, not just lip service."[12]

The technology community message boards are showing some increasing support as well. "Top marks to Big Blue for doing the right thing," says one member of slashdot.org.[13] "I applaud IBM for the fantastic software support of Linux. Not only for porting more apps to Linux but developing new ones altogether on the platform," says a member of the Temple of the Screaming Penguin, another technology site.[14]

Since 2000, Wladawsky-Berger has been surveying the technology community to gauge its needs. Linux is a customer-driven phenomenon that is shaping the future of computing, and Wladawsky-Berger's team has talked to thousands of developers, asking them how IBM can support them while simultaneously encouraging them to develop Linux-based programs.

Wladawsky-Berger speaks reverently of the community of Linux lovers that has grown exponentially; in interviews, he often defers to "the community" before formulating major strategic decisions. Technologically, IBM sees Linux as the operating system of choice for all of its software. Ten years ago, when IBM controlled the vast majority of mainframe systems, that would have been heresy, and programmers know it. IBM's change of heart has been consistently winning over the technology community.

"To be honest, we'd open source just about anything the [Linux] community wanted," he says.[15]

IBM is committed to embracing Linux across all of its product lines: Intel servers, Power-based servers, iSeries, mainframes, storage, OEM (original equipment manufacturer) technology, and everything in its $9 billion software group.

MAKING LARGE PORTIONS OF ITS INTELLECTUAL PROPERTY WIDELY AVAILABLE

At its core kernel, open source is just that: open. The computer code that powers Linux is available to programmers who would like to tinker with it, understand it, or improve it. On the other hand, the computer code that drives Microsoft Windows, for instance, is a company secret on the level of Coca-Cola's recipe.

Here's how Wladawsky-Berger describes it: "There is a very long tradition of researchers writing papers and publishing them openly. Their peers then read the papers, write additional papers on the topic, and everybody builds on everybody else's ideas.

"The sharing of this information, whether you're in a university, a research lab, or the private sector, is what advances research and innovation for the benefit of your community."[16]

With its Linux initiative, IBM is trying to build on that idea and avoid the traps other technology companies fall into of thinking they know what's best for the customer and that technology customers don't know what to ask for if it hasn't been invented yet.

Wladawsky-Berger says IBM has surveyed 2,700 customers and asked what they found appealing about Linux and where they're heading in the future. From those results, IBM has built its Linux strategy. Guy Kawasaki, CEO of Garage Technology Ventures and the father of evangelism marketing, loves this idea. "There's a fascination to how IBM can be evangelistic with Linux," he says.[17]

The irony is not lost on Wladawsky-Berger. As he told *Business 2.0* in 2001: "The Internet and Linux are far bigger than IBM."[18]

"IBM remains the most seriously committed vendor in the field around Linux," Gartner analyst George Weiss said in 2000. "They have the most to win, as well as the most to lose."[19]

EVANGELISM SCORECARD: IBM

Customer Plus-Delta

- Wladawsky-Berger spends most of his time visiting customers around the world.

Napsterize Your Knowledge

- IBM is making $40 million worth of software tools available for free to spur the development of additional Linux applications.

Build the Buzz

- IBM's bold program—$1 billion for promoting open source—created waves of buzz.
- "Peace/Love/Linux" guerilla marketing campaign made news for its hipness.

Create Community

- IBM is building goodwill among the existing community of open source developers by speaking at its conferences, providing tools, building information-packed Web sites for developers, and sending e-mail newsletters.

Bite-Size Chunks

- A number of IBM-created programs are free and available for downloading.

Create a Cause

- By throwing its considerable weight and influence behind Linux, IBM joins the open source movement.

Coordinates

Company:	IBM
Headquarters:	Armonk, New York
Founded:	1924
Chief executive:	Sam Palmisano
VP, technology strategy:	Irving Wladawsky-Berger
Description:	Hardware, software, and professional services
Industry:	Technology
Employees:	319,876
Ownership:	Publicly traded (NYSE: IBM)
Web site:	<www.ibm.com>

CUSTOMER EVANGELISM
WORKSHOP

*"In the arena of human life the honors and rewards fall to
those who show their good qualities in action."*

—ARISTOTLE

OK, so now what?

Creating customer evangelists for your organization requires planning, resources, and patience. The six tenets of customer evangelism marketing provide a framework to plan your customer activities. They are not steps to be performed in a specific order; rather, they are concepts to consider as your customer evangelism grows and matures.

To review, the tenets are:

- *Customer Plus-Delta.* Continuously understanding what your customers love about you and what they would like to see improved.
- *Napsterize your knowledge.* Sharing your intellectual capital in ways that are easily passed on to others.
- *Build the buzz.* Using natural networks that exist to get people talking.
- *Create community.* Finding ways to create a sense of belonging among your customers.
- *Bite-size chunks.* Developing easily digestible pieces for new evangelists.
- *Create a cause.* Rallying customers around something bigger than you.

In our seven case story companies, the tenets are applied differently and inventively. The Evangelism Scorecard at the end of each case story chapter provides ideas on how to apply the tenets to your business.

To help you consider this further, we have developed a series of questions to consider for each tenet.

CUSTOMER PLUS-DELTA

This is a great first step in your quest to create customer evangelists. Ask your current customers this series of open-ended questions to uncover more about who they are, how they feel about their relationship with you and your organization, and how they perceive the quality and value of your products and services.

- *What do current customers say that they love about you?* Listen to the emotion (or lack of it) to see if you are hitting the mark in delighting your customer base. You may be able to capture a few testimonials for your brochures.
- *What do they say you should specifically improve?* Customers evangelize products they feel are worthy to refer to friends and family. If you hear many negative answers to this question, perhaps a product overhaul is in order before continuing with your customer evangelism efforts.
- *What do customers value most about your company?* You may think it's the latest feature added to your product, but customers may say it's your telephone support. Ask customers to quantify the value of your products and services using real measures, if possible.
- *Do customers recommend you to others?* If so, how often? In what forums? Find out who your evangelists really are. Pay special attention to them—they are key to recruiting new customers.
- *What do customers say when they recommend you to others?* Pay close attention to the wording they use to describe you and why others should buy your product or service. This input can help refine your marketing communications.
- *Do you provide easy ways for your customers to regularly provide feedback?* Does your Web site make it easy for customers to enter suggestions for all areas of your business? Formally surveying your customers at regular intervals is good, but allowing customers to provide you with ongoing feedback is better.

NAPSTERIZE YOUR KNOWLEDGE

Napsterize parts of your organization, such as sharing intellectual capital and processes, to make them more valuable. Napsterize the obvious parts of your business that improve customer interaction or real-time data. Focus on innovating existing products and services that could become co-opted by Napsterization or commoditization.

- How can you become an information resource in your industry? How can you externalize internal company knowledge and expertise?
- Can you write an article on how to select a company like yours? Position your company as one that is looking out for its customers' best interests by helping them with the selection process instead of one that just wants to hand out its brochure.
- Can you fill your Web site with articles, book reviews, links to other resources, events lists, and so on around your specialty? Invite others to submit their suggestions for these things so you can post them for the good of the community.
- Can you package your knowledge to make it easily distributed?

For today's knowledge workers in industries such as consulting and technology, intellectual capital can be the company's most important asset. Keeping all expertise and knowledge bottled up inside the company doesn't help customers understand and spread the word about your core offerings.

BUILD THE BUZZ

Get people talking by creating buzz about your products and services. Leverage the natural networks in society and business to break through the clutter with infectious word of mouth.

- Do you know what the current buzz is regarding your products and services? Search the Internet, especially newsgroups and chat rooms, to see what people are saying.
- Can you identify the network hubs and megahubs for your industry? How many of these people do you have an existing relationship with?
- Are you nurturing relationships with these influencers? Do you offer them special access to your company? Do you feed them information about new products and services? Do you solicit their input?

- What is it about your product that's different? How can you make it stand out? Is there a story associated with your product?
- Are you selling products or experiences? Can you design a customer experience that will get people talking?
- Have you read the *Anatomy of Buzz* by Emanuel Rosen yet? We've given a quick sermon on Rosen's ideas, but pick up a copy of the buzz bible for yourself.

CREATE COMMUNITY

Help customers bond with you and each other by adding community programs to your marketing. Your current customer evangelists will help recruit new members into the community.

- Are customers already calling you to ask how they can meet other customers like themselves? Are customers already connecting to each other without you, via the Web perhaps?
- Ask customers to help develop a community program. Solicit their input and watch for the individuals who are eager to help. Can you appoint one as a leader of a specific program in your community-building efforts?
- Just try it and see what happens. Gather feedback from participants (and nonparticipants) all along the way. Let them shape your community program so that it provides value for all involved. Don't be afraid to end it if it's just not working.
- Can you hold a fun event to bring customers together to swap stories with other customers, à la Saturn Homecoming or Harley Owner Group rallies?
- Add community features, such as online bulletin boards, to your Web site. Create and moderate an e-mail discussion group to get customers to connect.
- Put a human face on your marketing. Feature your current evangelistic customers in your marketing communications efforts. Solicit testimonials and sprinkle them liberally throughout your Web site, brochures, and advertising.
- Create a special community program for your most evangelistic fans. Make them feel as though they are part of a select few who receive special benefits. Give these special few all the materials they need to spread the word for you. Embrace fan sites if you are lucky enough to have them.

BITE-SIZE CHUNKS

Break up your product or service portfolio into bite-size chunks, which introduces your company's products and services with small, easily consumed pieces. This strategy puts more of your product into the marketplace for people to experience and evangelize.

- For consumer commodities, give out samples of your products to network hubs. Ask them to introduce you to other network hubs to share samples with. Find communities where prospective customers gather and supply samples liberally.
- For technology products, can you offer a limited-time or limited-capacity trial version to prospective customers?
- For services companies, can you offer a "starter" version of service? Divide up your service portfolio into chunks that customers can bite off, one at a time.

CREATE A CAUSE

To show the world what you are really about, create a cause for your company. A good cause is meaningful; it is something that people—customers and employees—can believe in and rally around. When people believe in your cause, they'll evangelize you to others and recruit new believers into the fold. A cause need not be a charity to which you donate time or services; a cause can be a point around which your customers and employees rally—they support it and believe in it. Southwest Airlines and Harley-Davidson have built their company cultures and marketing strategies around the idea of freedom. No customer ever rallied for a company cause built around the notion of increased shareholder return.

- Is there a societal issue that affects your customer audience? What can you do to support a charitable cause that addresses this issue?
- Instead of just selling products, sell a dream. Think bigger about what would improve customers' lives, what would change your customers' world. Challenge yourself and your organization to think.

IS THIS THE END?

We've come to the end of this book, but we hope this is the beginning of a conversation. Our objective was to outline the six tenets of customer evangelism marketing and help you discover a new way to think about customers and marketing. The case story companies inspired us to write this book; we hope they inspire you to action.

Let us know how you are creating customer evangelists. Do you have a story about how you are doing this? Have you applied an idea from the book that was successful? Do you have some ideas to share with others? Join the customer evangelism community at <www.CreatingCustomerEvangelists.com>.

SPAM

creating customer vigilantes

Regular and consistently engaging e-mail communications with your customers and interested parties is an excellent and often-employed strategy to creating customer evangelists. If customers consider your e-mail communications like receiving personal letters from a friend, you are on the right path.

Because of its relative low cost and ease of use, e-mail marketing communications are also misused and abused. Too often, companies view e-mail as a customer acquisition tool, but it's not. It's a customer retention tool.

Yet the siren's song of e-mail marketers who promise untapped gold at the end of the Internet rainbow wails louder and louder. A client of ours received an unsolicited commercial e-mail about a broadcast e-mail program that promised to help them land new customers. Our client asked for advice: Should she take the offer or reject it? The company's pitch resonated like a beacon of possibility:

> If you send a Broadcast Email Advertisement to 50,000,000 People and Just 1 of 5,000 People Respond, You Can Generate 10,000 EXTRA ORDERS! How Much EXTRA PROFIT is this for You?

The pitch even calculated the math:

> Let's say you . . . Sell a $24.95 PRODUCT or SERVICE.

Let's say you . . . Receive JUST 1 ORDER for EVERY 2,500 EMAILS.

CALCULATION OF YOUR EARNINGS BASED ON THE ABOVE STATISTICS:

[Day 1]: $4,990 [Week 1]: $34,930 [Month 1]: $139,720

Research coming out of analyst firms such as Forrester, Jupiter, and eMarketer all tout e-mail marketing as a cost-effective way to reach customers. Like most offers than arrive unsolicited, this one is just like all the others: too good to be true.

This is not legitimate e-mail marketing. It's spam: nasty e-mail junk that increasingly fills up all of our in-boxes. Spammer companies like the one mentioned above and their unwitting customers are creating growing levels of "badwill." They erode the overall effectiveness of customer-centric e-mail communications. Ferris Research estimates that by 2003, the average business will have spent $400 per in-box deleting spam, compared to $55 in 2001.

Worse, spam creates the antithesis of the customer evangelist: the vigilante customer, who actively campaigns *against* you.

As a business owner or executive considering unsolicited broadcast e-mail as a marketing tactic, you can expect all sorts of results, and none include bags of easy money.

- *You will instantly anger a group of vocal activists.* Chances are that you will raise the ire of dozens or hundreds of anti-spam vigilantes. Their ranks are massive on the Internet. Send an unsolicited commercial e-mail to a vigilante without permission and you risk having that vigilante angrily call your business, flood your e-mail with hateful and vengeful responses, and report your company to the Federal Trade Commission.
- *Your name will be tarnished.* Other than bothering you at work, the vigilante may encourage others to do the same. The vigilante may append your company's name to online lists of "known spammers." People who didn't even receive your broadcast e-mail may send you angry e-mail, postal mail, and phone calls.
- *You may lose your e-mail services.* Sending spam through your Internet service provider (ISP) may cost you your Internet service. Spam clogs e-mail servers, sometimes crashes them, and otherwise causes headaches and complaints for an ISP. Your ISP would rather dump you than have to contend with those headaches.
- *You will have wasted your time chasing ghosts.* Some companies promise millions of e-mail addresses for your use. You may as well

write made-up up names and addresses on envelopes and send those through the U.S. Postal Service because it's the same principle. Most of the "millions" of e-mail addresses promised by spam merchants are computer-generated guesses based on deduction theory: ben@aol.com, ben1@aol.com, ben2@aol.com, and on into digital infinity.

That said, there are ways to grow your business and create customer evangelists through effective e-mail marketing:

1. Focus on building your own in-house e-mail list. If you offer different and unique products, create lists for each product.
2. Always request permission to send people e-mail. Always.
3. Make your e-mail communications relevant and anticipated. Tell people what they can expect from you.
4. Offer something of value. Offer a free white paper, product sample, hints and tips, etc.
5. Provide relevant content on an ongoing basis to a third party source. Is there a professional organization in your industry with a newsletter that your potential customers read? If your company provides IT consulting services, for instance, write a 250-500 word article for an association's monthly e-mail newsletter that goes out to 10,000 subscribers.

The true path to customer evangelism is paved with goodwill, and it never includes spam.

B

8 TIPS ON CREATING AN IDEAVIRUS FOR YOUR BUSINESS

When customers evangelize you to their friends and colleagues, what they say is as important as the passion behind their words. In short, are your evangelists pitching what you want prospects to hear?

To make it easy for customers to describe what you do, they must understand the idea of your company. It is, as author Seth Godin would say, an *ideavirus,* a concept that is easily communicated from one person to another. An ideavirus creates buzz, which contributes to the contagion of creating customer evangelists. This transfer of understanding must be:

- Easy
- Smooth
- Infectious

This is also known as the *elevator pitch,* or what you would say to a stranger about your value proposition (or someone else's) during the time it takes to ride 20 floors in an elevator. It's roughly equal to the attention span of most prospective customers in generating an interest in your product or service.

To create effective customer evangelists, your customers must know your elevator pitch as well as you do. How smooth is your company's pitch? Do people you meet nod knowingly when you describe your company's products or services, or do they look puzzled and ask you to explain more?

Here's how one of our clients turned quizzical looks into "Yes! I need your services now!"

ABC Technology Services (not the company's real name) asked for our help in landing new clients. Company executives described themselves approximately this way: "ABC designs and delivers network and systems management solutions that assist companies in cost-effectively maximizing the performance, up-time, and availability of their network infrastructures." From there, we undertook a three-step process.

Step 1. We interviewed ten of their current customers and asked them to talk about ABC's services in terms of value and how they would describe ABC's services to others. Understanding what customers say about you is integral to helping people spread the word.

It became clear that ABC's customers engaged the company during periods of crisis: computer systems were slow, e-mail was malfunctioning, or employees had to frequently reboot computers. ABC promptly fixed these problems and installed monitoring software to make sure these issues were history, not current events.

Step 2. Using the words of their customers, we reframed ABC's pitch to focus on the pain felt by prospective customers. Because ABC's primary source of leads was via word of mouth, we added a casual tone.

From "network and systems management," we changed the pitch to: "You know how when you are at work, and you are pulling your hair out because of computer problems? Your system is slow, you can't send or receive e-mail, or you have to reboot your computer a lot? Well, we fix those problems for businesses." We ditched the techie-talk in favor of simple language and a context that prospects could identify with: pain.

Step 3. The ABC executives tried the new pitch at a networking event. They were amazed at the profuse head nodding when delivering their new pitch. A failing computer system is a simple ideavirus to grasp, and it's easy for someone to tell others, as we saw demonstrated several times at the event. By the way, ABC landed six leads from this one event alone, by using their new and improved elevator pitch.

How do you create an ideavirus for your business? Try these eight tips:

1. Interview (or have a third party interview) your current satisfied customers.
2. Ask the customers to describe any pains or needs that first motivated them to buy your product or service.
3. Ask the customers to describe the value of your products or services.

4. Ask the customers how they would evangelize your business to others.
5. Write down exactly—word for word—the answers to these questions.
6. Reframe your pitch using the pain points of how customers would describe your services to others.
7. Test and refine your pitch at networking events.
8. Use your refined pitch in other marketing materials, such as your Web site or brochures.

MEASURING CUSTOMER EVANGELISM

A participant in one of our Creating Customer Evangelists workshops asked: How do you measure the success of customer evangelism marketing efforts?

Many a marketer throughout the annals of marketing history has struggled to measure the success of customer programs. To paraphrase the old adage by department store magnate John Wanamaker, "I know 50 percent of my marketing efforts are working. I just don't know which 50 percent." It's challenging, but not impossible. And the Internet constantly offers new measurement tools and tactics.

Our research has shown that customer evangelism marketing strategies improve customer loyalty and increase revenue from current customers. When organizations focus on customer relationships, they tend to build more loyal customers who purchase more frequently, and sometimes exclusively.

Customer evangelism marketing techniques also contribute to decreased customer acquisition costs because current, evangelistic customers recruit new customers on behalf of organizations they believe in.

To create metrics of success, first establish your current benchmarks:

- Number of current customers
- Customer retention rate (%)
- Revenue from repeat purchases of current customers

Measure these goals quarterly or annually. They are your big-picture organizational goals. To measure success among the six tenets of customer evangelism on a weekly, monthly or quarterly basis, try these metrics.

1. Customer Plus-Delta (continuously gather customer feedback).

- How many ideas for new products and services were gathered?
- How much revenue was generated by the new products and services?
- How many previously unknown problems were fixed based on customer feedback?
- How did the suggestions improve product quality?
- Did the suggestions help save money? If so, how much?

2. Napsterize your knowledge (share your knowledge freely).

- In how many places on the Internet is your company's expertise mentioned?
- In how many places online are your white papers posted?
- How many articles did you publish or have published?
- What is the referral or pass-along rate of your free e-mail newsletter?

3. Build the buzz (expertly tap into word-of-mouth networks).

- How did new and prospective customers say they discovered you? Ask for the specific place, press mention, or person. If it was a personal referral, what did the referrer say?
- Analyze traffic to your Web site. Which organizations visit the most?
- What types of organizations are they?
- Are they the ones you want visiting?
- What part of the world are they from?
- Which parts of the site do they visit most?
- How are people discovering your site? Most Web site traffic analysis tools can measure search terms entered into search engines that brought visitors to your site.

4. Create community (encourage your customers to meet and share information).

- How many customers are on your e-mail list?
- How is your subscriber rate trending: increasing, decreasing, or flat?
- How many customer events have you held? How many guests did customers bring? How many of those guests became customers?

5. Make bite-size chunks (devise specialized, smaller offerings to get customers to bite).

- How many different product or service offerings make up your portfolio?
- How many of those offerings have you divided into sample offerings?
- How many prospects have sampled your product or service?
- How many prospects turned into customers?
- What's the referral rate of people who sampled your offering and told others?

6. Create a cause (focus on making the world, or an industry, better).

- How many people contact you because they believe in your cause?
- How many of them became customers?
- How many customers say they purchase from you exclusively because of what you stand for?
- How many people send their resumes asking to work in your organization because they believe in what you do or what you stand for?

Employ these metrics for several quarters or a year, then revisit the big-picture benchmark metrics and compare the previous numbers. If you have maintained a high level of quality and consistently execute well, your big-picture numbers should be at least 5 percent higher.

Evangelism marketers steadfastly believe that doing the right thing for customers will pay dividends ten-fold in the form of repeat purchases and customers who buy because of the word of others.

HOW TO SPOT EVANGELISTS AND WHAT TO DO WITH THEM

People talk about you. They talk about your company, your products and services, and your personality. Many say nice things, and some are absolutely gushy with their praise. Would you like to know who they are? How do you find your evangelists?

Short of spy cams and hidden microphones, it's not difficult to find your evangelists. Here are a few ideas.

Scan the Web using your favorite search engine and discover where you are mentioned online and by whom. Make note of everyone who compliments your products and services and everyone who criticizes them. For the people who love you, send them a hand-written thank-you note. Invite them in to a special club with other evangelists where they get inside information about products and services. Make them feel extra special. For those who take issue with you products or services, find a way to contact them via e-mail or ask if it's OK to talk on the phone. The difference between an unhappy customer and an evangelist is often just a phone call. More than anything, unhappy customers just want to be *heard and acknowledged*. Grant an unhappy customer that wish.

Ask prospective customers specifically how they discovered you. If it was from a friend or colleague, ask the prospect for the name of the referrer. Keep detailed records of how people discovered you. With some of our clients, we create a Buzz Map, which illustrates the actual routes of how they landed customers via word of mouth. A map of customer connections quickly illuminates your biggest evangelists.

If you have an opt-in e-mail list, add a field that asks how people discovered you. Continually refine the quantifiable nature of this field. You want to gather as much information as possible from this field, especially if the referrals are from people. Those are your evangelists!

Be an active participant in e-mail discussion lists and online bulletin boards that your customers frequent. Watch for customers who post recommendations about you. Cultivate relationships with them. Keep them in your loop.

Use Web site tracking software to understand how Web site visitors discover you. If customers, prospects, fans, or evangelists link to your site, do *not* send them a cease-and-desist letter. This creates customer vigilantes, not customer evangelists. Do *not* let your corporate counsel argue that fan sites contribute to brand dilution. This is pure crap espoused by prosecutorial-minded lawyers intent on making customers play by ridiculous notions of trademark protection. (Note: Protect your trademarks against *competitors,* not customers.) Encourage links to your site, wherever fans would like to create them. Provide fans with pictures of your products, logos, movies, animations—anything that makes them feel connected to you. *They are your volunteer sales force.*

So you have spotted an evangelist who sings your praises to others. Now what? If strategy is also comprised of what *not* to do, here's a story.

In an online discussion forum in 2002, someone asked for a recommendation of a Web-based event registration service. We have been pleased with the service we have used for the events we host, so we posted a complimentary recommendation to the forum. We outlined the service's strong points and mentioned just one weak point: no post-event reporting that outlines all fees deducted from the total proceeds.

The next day I received an e-mail from the director of product support at the registration company:

Jackie,

Thanks for posting the nice message. We have ear marked several areas for improvement and are releasing a new version to the system soon that we think you will like very much. I did want to add something re: one comment . . . 'Only weak point: reports of actual transactions and fees is sparse.'

I was surprised to see this. While we are aware of things we need to work on, reporting and revenue/transactional reporting is extremely strong in our system. I just wanted to mention this, so you can be aware of these features before you use the system again. There are custom download functions that allow you to create your own download report formats. We have monthly revenue reports in simple format. There are downloadable revenue reports. Plus you can view and download detailed accounting reports (with all line items included).

Before you use the system next, feel free to set up an appointment with me, and I'll walk you through these features. I think these will be of tremendous use.

I had evangelized this company's service to 3,300 people on an e-mail discussion list. Instead of asking to determine my concerns, he took issue with my comment, assumed that it was my error and pressed me to get some training. In essence, he said, "Thanks for saying nice things about us to a lot of people for free, but, damnit, get it right!"

That said, here are five tips on what to do when you spot an evangelist in the wild:

1. *Immediately contact the evangelist.* Thank her profusely. If you don't personally know the person, call her. Find out more about her business, her challenges, and her personal interests.
2. *If they say something you wish they hadn't, pick up the phone and call.* If you only have an e-mail address, request a phone conversation. Be genuinely inquisitive in understanding their issues. Don't chastise customers for saying something you perceive to be wrong.
3. *Put the person on your list of evangelists for a future opportunity to thank them in a more special way.* A simple rule of thumb: Don't treat your customers like a socialist country where everyone is equally important. Your evangelists deserve special treatment. The best treatment is attention, not necessarily discounts or coupons.
4. *Reward your evangelists unexpectedly.* If your evangelists contact you to purchase additional products or services, provide extra value. Send a book. Hand them an extra set of football tickets. Introduce them to your CEO and/or president.
5. *Develop a formal evangelist program that periodically rewards all of your evangelists.* Host an annual party and invite only the evangelists. Take your best evangelists to lunch every quarter.

Remember, customer evangelism is a gift. It's the highest form of customer loyalty. Your evangelists must be treated like the royalty they are.

ENDNOTES

Chapter 1 | **Customer Evangelism: A Manifesto**

1. Southwest Airlines provided the authors with a packet of letters it received after September 11, 2001.

2. Ann McGee-Cooper, telephone interview with authors, 15 March 2002.

3. Jennifer Disabatino, "Report: Job Cuts in 2001 Reach Nearly 2 million," *Computerworld,* 3 January, 2002.

4. Data on publicly traded bankruptcy filings provided by BankruptcyData .com <bankruptcydata.com>.

5. Eric S. Raymond, *The Cathedral and the Bazaar.* (Sebastopol, California: O'Reilly, 2001), 177.

6. "Let's All Blame the Marketing Director," MP3 and lyrics on Harpell .com <www.harpell.com/results>.

7. David Shenk, *Data Smog.* (San Francisco: Harper, 1997), 30.

8. EuroRSCG, "Wired & Wireless: High-Tech Capitols Now and Next," 2001 <www.wiredandwireless.eurorscg.com>.

Chapter 2 | **When Customers Believe**

1. Guy Kawasaki, interview with authors, Palo Alto, California, 2 February 2002.

2. Ibid.

3. Ibid.

4. George Silverman, *Secrets of Word-of-Mouth Marketing: How to Trigger Exponential Sales through Runaway Word of Mouth.* (New York: AMACOM, 2001), 15–16.

5. Kim Girard, "The Return of the Crummy Job," *Business 2.0,* 6 February 2001.

6. Tim Sanders, interview with authors, Chicago, 25 February 2002.

7. K.C. Swanson, "The Joy of Pepsi," *TheStreet.com*, 18 April 2001.

Chapter 3 | Customer Plus-Delta: Understanding the Love

1. "Using Complaints for Quality Assurance Decisions," TARP, 1997 <www.e-satisfy.co.uk/research2.asp>.

2. Jackie Sloan, telephone interview with authors, 2 April 2002.

3. Chicago Public Radio (WBEZ) research study, March 2002.

4. Ibid.

5. Michael Totty, "Information, Please: How three companies are using the Web to find out more about their customers—or to let their customers know more about them," *Wall Street Journal*, 29 October 2001.

6. Alex Johnston, telephone interview with authors, 2 April 2002.

7. Maxine Clark, telephone and e-mail interviews with authors, February–April 2002.

Chapter 4 | Napsterize Your Knowledge: Give to Receive

1. Stewart Brand, *The Media Lab: Inventing the Future at MIT.* (Viking Penguin, 1987).

2. Editorial, "Waiting to Be Napsterized?" *National Underwriter Life & Health/Financial Services Edition Online*, 5 February 2001 <www.nunews.com /lifeandhealth/editorials/020501/L200106waiting.asp>.

3. Joel Selvin, "Did Napster Help Boost Record Sales?" *San Francisco Chronicle*, 5 August 2001.

4. Peter Rojas, "Fabulous Do-It-Yourself Manufacturing: Xerox never duplicated like this," *Red Herring*, 1 May 2001.

5. Massachusetts Institute of Technology, "MIT to Make Nearly All Course Materials Available Free on the World Wide Web," MIT press release, 4 April 2001 <web.mit.edu/newsoffice/nr/2001/ocw.html>.

Chapter 5 | Build the Buzz: Spreading the Word

1. Emanuel Rosen, interview with authors, Palo Alto, California, 6 February 2002.

2. Ibid.

3. Ibid.

4. "Cuban calls out NBA's director of officiating," ESPN.com, 7 January 2001 <espn.go.com/nba/news/2002/0107/1307127.html>.

5. Mark Cuban, interview with authors, Dallas, 20 January 2002.

6. Ibid.

7. Gerry Khermouch, "Buzz Marketing," *BusinessWeek*, 30 July 2001 <www.businessweek.com/magazine/content/01_31/b3743001.htm>.

8. John Gaffney, "The Cool Kids Are Doing It. Should You?" *Business 2.0*, October 2001 <www.business2.com/articles/mag/0,1640,17380,FF.html>.

9. Joseph Pine II and James H. Gilmore, *The Experience Economy.* (Boston: Harvard Business School Press, 1999).

10. Ibid.

11. Renee Dye, "The Buzz on Buzz," *Harvard Business Review,* November–December 2000.

12. Tim Sanders, interview with authors, Chicago, 25 February 2002.

13. Richard Dawkins, *The Selfish Gene.* (Oxford University Press, 1990).

Chapter 6 | Create Community: Bringing Customers Together

1. Daryl Urquhart, telephone interview with authors, 2 April 2002.

2. Melanie Wells, "Cult Brands," *Forbes,* 16 April 2001.

3. Heath Row, telephone interview with authors, 28 February 2002.

4. Ibid.

5. Ibid.

6. Ibid.

7. Ibid.

8. Erich Joachimsthaler and David Aaker, "Building Brands without Mass Media," *Harvard Business Review,* January-February issue, 1997.

9. Full Circle Consulting <www.fullcirc.com>. Find the Online Facilitation e-mail discussion list at <groups.yahoo.com/group/onlinefacilitation>.

10. Lisa M. Bowman, "Warner Bros. Backs Off Harry Potter Fight," News.com, 16 March 2001.

11. Marc Weingaten, "LOTR: The Fellowship of the Web," *Business 2.0,* January 2002.

Chapter 7 | Bite-Size Chunks: From Sampling to Evangelism

1. The Quotations Page <www.quotationspage.com/quotes/Henry_Ford/>.

2. Sampling statistics from James P. Santella & Associates <www.santella.com/marketing.htm#RESULTS%20OF%20BRAND%20MARKETING%202001%20SURVEY>.

3. Gerald Haman, interview with authors, Chicago, 12 October 2001.

4. Matt Fitzgerald, interview with authors, Dallas, 29 January 2002.

Chapter 8 | Create a Cause: When Business Is Good

1. Guy Kawasaki, *Selling the Dream: How to Promote Your Product, Company, or Ideas—and Make a Difference—Using Everyday Evangelism.* (New York: Harper Business, 1992), 4.

2. Guy Kawasaki, interview with authors, Palo Alto, California, 2 February 2002.

3. Kawasaki, *Selling the Dream,* 14.

4. Richard Cross and Janet Smith, *Customer Bonding: 5 Steps to Lasting Customer Loyalty.* (Lincolnwood, IL: NTC Business Books, 1995), 95.

5. Sue Atkins, "The Wider Benefits of Backing a Good Cause," *Marketing,* 9 September 1999 <www.psaresearch.com/bib4314.html>.

6. Business in the Community <www.bitc.org.uk/marketing.html>.

7. Carol Cone, "Cause Branding in the 21st Century," Public Service Advertising Research Center, 1998 <www.psaresearch.com/causebranding .html>.

8. Harvey Meyer, "When the Cause Is Just," *Journal of Business Strategy,* November–December 1999 <www.psaresearch.com/bib4313.html>.

9. Dan Pallotta, interview with authors, Los Angeles, 13 February 2002.

10. Brian Erwin, interview with authors, 22 March 2002.

11. Maxine Clark, "Putting the Heart Back in Retailing," Texas A&M Retailing Issues Letter, January 2001, Volume 13, Number 1.

Chapter 9 | Hot Marketing Now: Krispy Kreme Doughnuts

1. Stan Parker, telephone interview by authors, 5 March 2002.

2. Dan Voorhis, "Up All Night for a Sweet Sunup Treat," *The Wichita Eagle,* 5 December, 2001.

3. Dennis Pollock, "Krispy Crazy: Opening of a doughnut shop in north Fresno ignites a feeding frenzy and a media blitz," *The Fresno Bee,* 1 August, 2001.

4. Lisa Victoria Martinez, "Kreme de la Crème of fans," *Denver Post,* 28 March, 2001.

5. Kathy Mulday, "Countdown Begins for Krispy Kreme's Arrival," *Seattle Post-Intelligencer,* 1 August, 2001.

6. Tim Schooley, "Krispy Kreme Franchise Rolls to Town," *Pittsburgh Business Times,* 19 June, 2000.

7. Dennis R. Getto, "A Brief History of the Doughnut," *Milwaukee Journal Sentinel,* 12 December, 2001.

8. Candy Sagon, "The Hole Story: How the Great American Doughnut Took Shape," *Washington Post,* 6 March, 2002.

9. Parker, interview.

10. Ibid.

11. Ibid.

12. Ibid.

13. Ibid.

14. Scott Hume, "Model Behavior: Krispy Kreme's Scott Livengood enjoys dozens of hot opportunities," *Restaurants and Institutions,* 1 July, 2001.

15. Parker, interview.

16. Material provided by Krispy Kreme.

17. Parker, interview.

18. Hume, *Restaurants and Institutions.*

19. Parker, interview.

20. Ibid.

21. Ibid.

22. Ibid.

23. Karen Mishra, telephone interview with authors, 7 March, 2002.
24. Parker, interview.
25. Mishra, interview.
26. Parker, interview.

Chapter 10 | High-Flying Solution: SolutionPeople

1. Gerald Haman, interviews with authors, Chicago, various dates, October 2001–May 2002.
2. Ibid.
3. Ibid.
4. Ibid.
5. Ibid.
6. Ibid.
7. Ibid.
8. Ibid.
9. Ibid.
10. Ibid.
11. Kevin Olsen, interview with authors, Downers Grove, Illinois, 12 March, 2002.
12. Ibid.
13. Haman, interview.

Chapter 11 | The History Lessons of O'Reilly's Wars: O'Reilly & Associates

1. Tim O'Reilly, interview with authors, Sebastopol, California, 6 February, 2002.
2. Evelyn S. McClure, *Sebastopol, California: History, Homes, and People,* 1995, Belleview Press.
3. Simon Heseltine, "The Crimean War (1865-56)," <mo.essortment .com/thecrimeanwar_rezc.html>.
4. <tim.oreilly.com>
5. O'Reilly, interview.
6. <tim.oreilly.com>
7. O'Reilly, interview.
8. Ibid.
9. Ibid.
10. Sara Winge, interview with authors, Sebastopol, California, 7 February, 2002 and via e-mail, various dates.
11. O'Reilly, interview.
12. Ibid.
13. Ibid.
14. Ibid.
15. Jeff "Hemos" Bates, e-mail interview with authors, various dates, 25 March, 2002–15 April, 2002.
16. Brian Erwin, telephone interview with authors, 22 March, 2002.

17. Ibid.

18. O'Reilly, interview.

19. Ibid.

20. Erwin, interview.

21. Ibid.

22. Erwin, interview.

23. O'Reilly, interview.

24. Simone Paddock, telephone interview with authors, 10 August, 2001.

25. O'Reilly, interview.

26. Ibid.

27. Ibid.

28. Ibid.

29. Ibid.

30. Ibid.

31. Ibid.

32. Ibid.

Chapter 12 | The New Mavericks of Marketing: The Dallas Mavericks

1. Mark Cuban, interviews with authors, Dallas, Texas, and via e-mail, various dates, 30 January, 2002–15 April 2002.

2. Jaime Aron, "Sweet Revenge: Billionaire Mavericks owner dishes ice cream," Associated Press, January 16, 2002.

3. Kevin B. Blackistone, "Calling a Bluff: What's Cuban's number?" *The Dallas Morning News,* January 19, 2002.

4. Cuban, interview.

5. Ibid.

6. Ibid.

7. Rick Alm, interview with authors, Dallas, Texas, 30 January, 2002.

8. Todd Walley, interview with authors, Dallas, Texas, 29 January, 2002.

9. Chris Bontrager, interview with authors, Dallas, Texas, 29 January, 2002.

19. George Killebrew, interview with authors, Dallas, Texas, 29 January, 2002.

11. Alm, interview.

12. Ibid.

13. Cuban, interview.

14. Ibid.

15. Ibid.

16. Ibid.

17. George Prokos, interview with authors, Dallas, Texas, 29 January, 2002.

18. Shawn Bradley, e-mail interview with authors, 17 April, 2002.

19. Greg Buckner, e-mail interview with authors, 17 April, 2002.

20. Cuban, interview.

21. Cuban, interview.

22. Matt Fitzgerald, interviews with authors, Dallas, Texas, via telephone and e-mail, various dates, 29 January, 2002–27 June, 2002.

23. Ibid.

24. Ibid.

25. Ibid.

26. Ibid.

27. Cuban, interview.

28. Ibid.

29. Ibid.

30. Ibid.

31. Ibid.

32. Bradley, interview.

33. Buckner, interview.

34. Prokos, interview.

35. Cuban, interview.

Chapter 13 | A Bear Market for Retailing: Build-A-Bear Workshop

1. Maxine Clark, interviews with authors via telephone and e-mail, various dates, 22 February, 2002–20 April, 2002.

2. Robert Berner, Gerry Khermouch and Aixa Pascual, "Retail Reckoning: There are just too many stores. Warning: Big shakeout ahead," *BusinessWeek*, December 10, 2001.

3. Cheryl Hall, "The Right Stuff: Creator of Build-A-Bear Workshop finds success by remaining a child at heart," *The Dallas Morning News*, October 22, 2000.

4. Teresa F. Lindeman, "Former Payless Chief Hits Pay Dirt with Build-A-Bear," *Pittsburgh Post-Gazette*, August 3, 2001

5. Clark, interview.

6. Ibid.

7. Ibid.

8. Ibid.

9. Ibid.

10. Ibid.

11. Ibid.

12. Ibid.

13. Ibid.

14. <www.theacsi.org>

15. Clark, interview.

16. Teresa Kroll, telephone interview with authors, 26 February, 2002.

17. Ibid.

18. Clark, interview.

19. Ibid.

20. Ibid.

21. Ibid.

22. Ibid.

23. Kroll, interview.

24. Mel Duvall, "Top 10 Companies to Work For," *Interactive Week,* April 9, 2001.

25. Kroll, interview.

26. Clark, interview.

27. Ibid.

28. Ibid.

29. Kroll, interview.

30. Ibid.

31. Ibid.

32. Ibid.

33. Clark, interview.

Chapter 14 | A Cause, Not Just an Airline: Southwest Airlines

1. Kim Clark, "Nothing But the Plane Truth," *U.S. News & World Report,* 31 December 2001.

2. From a packet of letters the company provided to the authors.

3. Jim Parker, comments made during "Message to the Field" employee meeting in Chicago, Illinois, 25 March 2002.

4. Ibid.

5. "Air Herb's Secret Weapon," *Chief Executive,* 1999, <chiefexecutive .net/mag/146/article1.htm>.

6. "The Fallen," *BusinessWeek,* 14 January 2002 <www.businessweek.com /magazine/content/02_02/b3765055.htm>.

7. "Flight Attendants Can Be Humorous, Too," <www.lovedungeon.net /humor/misc/attendants.html>.

8. *Chief Executive.*

9. Parker, comments.

10. Linda Rutherford, interview with authors, Dallas, Texas, 30 January 2002.

11. Kevin Krone, interview with authors, Dallas, Texas, 30 January 2002.

12. Parker, comments.

13. John Huey, "The Jack and Herb Show," *eCompany,* January 1999.

14. *Chief Executive.*

15. Herb Kelleher, "A Culture of Commitment," *Leader to Leader,* Spring 1997.

16. <www.iflyswa.com/help/luvbook.html>

17. Clark, "Nothing But the Plane Truth."

18. Rich Marcotte, telephone interview with authors, 7 March 2002.

19. Parker, comments.

20. Patty Kryscha, interview with authors, Chicago, Illinois 18 February 2002.

21. Ibid.

22. Ibid.

Chapter 15 | **The Billion-Dollar Cause: IBM**

1. Robert McMillan, "Friendly, Big and Blue: In a world of upstarts, is IBM becoming Linux's father figure?" Linux Magazine, October 2000 <www.linux-mag.com/2000-10/ibm_01.html>.

2. <www.linux10.org/history>

3. Joe Wilcox, "IBM to Spend $1 Billion on Linux in 2001," News.com, 12 December 2000 <news.com.com/2100-1001-249750.html?legacy=cnet>.

4. Eric S. Raymond, *The Cathedral and the Bazaar.* (Sebastopol, California: O'Reilly, 2001).

5. Jeff "Hemos" Bates, e-mail interview with authors, various dates 25 March 2002–15 April 2002.

6. McMillan, "Friendly, Big and Blue."

7. Photo of "Peace. Love. Linux" street campaign by Rich Hein. Reprinted with special permission from the *Chicago Sun-Times.* Copyright 2002.

8. Mary Jo Foley, "IBM's Palmisano touts Linux at confab," News.com, 31 January 2001 <news.com.com/2009-1001-251809.html?legacy=cnet>.

9. Tim O'Reilly, interviews with authors, 6 February–2 April 2002.

10. Spencer E. Ante, "Big Blue's Big Bet on Free Software," Business Week, 10 December 2001 <www.businessweek.com/magazine/content/01_50/b3761094.htm>.

11. Bates, interview.

12. O'Reilly, interview.

13. <slashdot.org/articles/01/02/13/0254220.shtml>

14. <screaming-penguin.com>

15. McMillan, "Friendly, Big and Blue."

16. Irving Wladawsky-Berger, speech to IBM Technical Developer Conference, San Francisco, August 2001 <www.ibm.com/news/us/2001/08/15.html>.

17. Guy Kawasaki, interview with authors, 8 February 2002.

18. William J. Holstein, "Big Blue Wages Open Warfare," *Business 2.0,* April 2001 <www.business2.com/articles/mag/0,1640,14645%7C2,FF.html>.

19. Wilcox, "IBM to spend $1 billion on Linux in 2001."

REFERENCES

Cialdini, Robert B. *Influence: The Psychology of Persuasion*. Rev. ed. New York: William Morrow, 1993.

Cross, Richard, and Janet Smith. *Customer Bonding: 5 Steps to Lasting Customer Loyalty*. Lincolnwood, Illinois: NTC Business Books, 1995.

Dawkins, Richard. *The Selfish Gene*. Oxford: Oxford University Press, 1990.

Giovagnoli, Melissa and Jocelyn Carter-Miller. *Networlding: Building Relationships for Opportunities and Success*. San Francisco: Jossey-Bass, 2000.

Gladwell, Malcolm. *The Tipping Point: How Little Things Can Make a Big Difference*. Boston: Little, Brown and Company, 2000.

Godin, Seth. *Unleashing the Ideavirus*. Do You Zoom, Inc., 2000.

Godin, Seth. *Permission Marketing*. New York: Simon & Schuster, 1999.

Kawasaki, Guy. *Rules for Revolutionaries: The Capitalist Manifesto for Creating and Marketing New Products and Services*. HarperBusiness, 1999.

Kawasaki, Guy. *Selling the Dream: How to Promote Your Product, Company, or Ideas—and Make a Difference—Using Everyday Evangelism*. New York: HarperCollins, 1991.

Kotler, Philip. *Marketing Management: Analysis, Planning, Implementation & Control*. 10th ed. Englewood Cliffs, New Jersey: Prentice Hall, 1991.

Kotler, Philip, and Gary Armstrong. *Principles of Marketing*. 5th ed. Englewood Cliffs, New Jersey: Prentice Hall, 1991.

McClure, Evelyn S. *Sebastopol, California: History, Homes, and People, 1855–1920*. Belle View Press, 1995.

Pallotta, Dan. *When Your Moment Comes: A Guide to Fulfilling Your Dreams by a Man Who Has Led Thousands to Greatness.* San Diego, California: Jodere Group, 2001

Pine, Joseph, and James H. Gilmore. *The Experience Economy.* Boston: Harvard Business Review Press, 1999.

Pink, Daniel P. *Free Agent Nation: How America's New Independent Workers Are Transforming the Way We Live.* New York: Warner, 2001.

Porter, Michael E. *Competitive Strategy.* New York: Free Press, 1980.

Raymond, Eric S. *The Cathedral and the Bazaar.* Sebastopol, California: O'Reilly, 2001.

Reichheld, Frederick F. *The Loyalty Effect.* Boston: Harvard Business School Press, 1996.

Reichheld, Frederick F. *Loyalty Rules!* Boston: Harvard Business School Press, 2001

Rosen, Emanuel. *The Anatomy of Buzz: How to Create Word of Mouth Marketing.* New York: Currency Doubleday, 2000.

Seybold, Patrica B., and Ronni T. Marshak. *Customers.com: How to Create a Profitable Business Strategy for the Internet and Beyond.* New York: Times Business, 1998.

Shenk, David. *Data Smog.* Harper San Francisco. 1998 (revised).

Silverman, George. *Secrets of Word-of-Mouth Marketing: How to Trigger Exponential Sales through Runaway Word of Mouth.* New York: AMACOM, 2001.

Sanders, Tim. *Love Is the Killer App.* New York: Crown Business, 2002.

Siegel, David. *Futurize Your Enterprise: Business Strategy in the Age of the E-Customer.* New York: John Wiley & Sons, 1999.

INDEX